In the comprehensive way of life embraced by the spiritual traditions of Aboriginal peoples in North and South America, the habits of animals teach humans about wholeness and their role within the web of life. My readings and knowledge are entirely inadequate to qualify me as anything but a wanderer. But aspects of two animals have helped me to clarify some issues in my own life. I include them in the title because it turns out that these aspects, as I understand them, echo throughout the book.

Dragonfly clears the way to understanding our real identities and true paths by helping us to see through illusions. Turtle teaches us to become grounded so that we can live more fully in the present and open ourselves to deeper sources of insight and creativity. Together, they show us how to see ourselves and our relationship with life as if for the first time.

Author's Note: I've made every effort to locate and acknowledge originators and sources for the short quotations contained in this book. I apologize in advance for any oversights.

National Library of Canada Cataloguing in Publication Data

Bernardi, Dennis
    Dragonflies and turtles : a guide to living in the hurri-
cane's eye /
Dennis Bernardi.
Includes bibliographical references.
ISBN 1-55395-884-5
    I. Title.
BF637.S4B473 2003   158.1   C2003-901143-7

This book was published *on-demand* in cooperation with Trafford Publishing. On-demand publishing is a unique process and service of making a book available for retail sale to the public taking advantage of on-demand manufacturing and Internet marketing. **On-demand publishing** includes promotions, retail sales, manufacturing, order fulfilment, accounting and collecting royalties on behalf of the author.

Suite 6E, 2333 Government St., Victoria, B.C. V8T 4P4, CANADA
Phone   250-383-6864   Toll-free   1-888-232-4444 (Canada & US)
Fax   250-383-6804   E-mail   sales@trafford.com
Web site   www.trafford.com   TRAFFORD PUBLISHING IS A DIVISION OF TRAFFORD HOLDINGS LTD.
Trafford Catalogue #03-0247   www.trafford.com/robots/03-0247.html

10   9   8   7   6   5   4   3   2   1

DRAGONFLIES
&
TURTLES

A Guide to Living in
the Hurricane's Eye

Dennis Bernardi

DEDICATION

This book is dedicated to my wife Lynda, my daughter Leigh, my son Aaron, my sister Lita and my parents Clara and Bruno.

ACKNOWLEDGEMENTS

Thanks to my wife Lynda for the support, suggestions and infinite patience during the highs and lows; to Kathy and Alan Aylett, and the Bernardis - Aaron, Leigh, Lita and Lynda - for road-testing the book, kicking the tires and providing invaluable feedback and encouragement; to Bob Boegel, for parachuting in and rescuing me from the computer weeds that I allowed to accumulate; to John Butler, for all manner of poetics and instigations; to Hattie Luke-Maher, for humble wisdom; to Andrew Warren, for giving it life through graphic design; and to Father Charles Gonet, for keeping me from drowning in my own juices so many years ago.

"The real voyage of discovery consists not in seeking new landscapes, but in having new eyes"

Marcel Proust

I hope you enjoy "Dragonflies,"

Lorna!

Dennis Bernardi

CONTENTS

CONTENTS

Introduction

This primitive book was pieced together by a fragmented mind whose efforts to get out of its own way has been a jerky trip between extremes and toward light that often turns out to be an approaching train. Lurching from excess seriousness about the world to hopelessness and trying not to give a damn, from manic creativity and production to exhaustion and disillusionment - and back again - my history is crowded with crowding: squeezing too many activities onto congested agendas filled with responsibility, striving, learning new stuff while trying to keep up with accelerating demands possessing foggy purpose. The book is probably an attempt to teach what I most need to learn.

I suspect I'm not alone. Blind busy-ness is a form of violence that smothers perspective, peace of mind and wisdom. The world trains us to run and try to catch up. It also tells us that time is in short supply and that there isn't any left over for our nourishment. We also shuffle through mountains of useless information every day while trying to ignore the financial and job insecurity promoted by our economic system. The corporate monotony of our main thoroughfares can hypnotize us. Horror and violence are big business. Our main job is to buy and consume it. Numbed, we may hardly notice the erosion of our creative energies.

Our society accepts idleness and play only as periodic refreshers that enable us to work harder in order to meet external demands. We can end up feeling like hamsters on a wheel and put more faith in the forces that keep us running than in ourselves. Exhausted, we complete tasks but feel empty because there are so many more to accomplish and we're not sure about the *why* of them.

We can begin to change this exhausting arrangement as soon as we accept the notion that self-worth and survival do not depend solely on earning points through racing or even accomplishment in the world. It is also unconditional as our birthright

The Chinese sage Lao Tzu pointed out that the wheel is most itself at the hub, the pot is most itself where the emptiness is and the room is most itself where the space is. We create this space when we pause, rest and let go of accumulated garbage in its many forms. We are meant to move in the space between stillness and passion. Without it, we cease to be ourselves and, irrespective of worldly accomplishments, become flat tires, filled pots and congested rooms.

We always have the freedom to step outside the hamster's cage (it's unlocked) and see the process of our lives from a place that allows us clarity. We can become observers who detach from those forces of speed and noise that provide only small, quick details with no apparent connection to each other or a bigger picture. We can distance ourselves from the daily pressures to fit in and automatically accept pre-cooked formulas, experts, easy answers and the quick thrills of the global-franchise marketplace. We can choose how we will live our lives.

Who is the Book For?

This is not a time management book. It does not show you how to re-distribute the load so that you can squeeze more into less time. It offers no self-help program for total self-mastery that exposes your hidden genius and the secrets of total domination. It even refuses to reveal the secret path to mega-living leading toward the crossroads at perfection's gate.

It's about much less than that.

The book is for people who fear they are not living according to an inner compass, who feel their lives are being dictated from somewhere outside themselves and whose depleted energies are devoted to hanging on for someone else's ride. It's for people grown tired of seeing reality in jagged pieces and who want to pay more attention to their own needs, dreams and relationships.

As compelling as outside forces may be, we remain the custodians of our own voices and our relationship with the world around us. We can stabilize ourselves by relying less on outside pressure and our roles in responding to it, and more on who we are and where our passions and values lead us. We can line up our outer existence with our inner voice by conditioning ourselves to step back regularly and view our own paths with clarity and perspective. From that quiet place we can re-enter the world better able to experience it with commitment that grows from inside.

So the book is about less rather than more. Its job is to help you remove deadweight and quit, destroy, kick out, banish, exile and give the heave-ho to some of the preoccupations that get in the way of connecting to that which has value for you. This cannot be done passively. It requires discernment, discipline and irreverence.

What's In It?

The book is organized into five chapters, each consisting of several short, related pieces addressing themes that have held importance for me and that I hope will be of practical value for you.

Chapter One: Step Back and See the Bars on the Cage explores the need to develop perspective and insight into the forms of acid that can eat away confidence and dominate our energies. These stressors include but go beyond speed and are so soaked into our daily lives that we may hardly notice them.

Chapter Two: Stop the World and Get Off recognizes the need to pull over to the side of the road, pause and be aware of our lives as we live them. It provides ideas and activities for moving away from obsession with the past and future, and connecting to the present moment, the only place where life can be fully lived.

Chapter Three: Quit Junk and Travel Light provides a starting point for creating more breathing room in your life. It presents six simple steps for simplifying your surroundings by getting rid of possessions that may be getting in your way.

Chapter Four: Give Yourself the Time and Space to Process Your Life offers alternative ways to view time so that it serves you. It presents ideas and tips for carving out more time and space to live creatively.

Chapter Five: Connect and Share describes how our emergence from distraction can produce new perspective on the spiritual reality of giving and receiving in our daily lives. When I began drafting the book, I didn't foresee the loudness with which spirituality would emerge in the script. It even got its own chapter. As in our daily lives, so in the book – it's proven to be unavoidable.

Sources and Selected Bibliography lists some key sources for those readers who wish to explore the book's themes more deeply.

How To Use It

While the book provides some tools for stripping away various forms of accumulated garbage and freeing up energy for more important things, the reader's life experience is the only authority that counts. I hope the book turns out to be a resource that helps you exercise that authority without having to wrestle with mind-numbing programs and techniques. I am not presenting a " system for living " and have tried to avoid laying out comfortable homilies as insulation against life's cold winds. If I say it right, you will recognize it. And if it has enough importance for you, you will know what to do with it.

Some people prefer logic, structure and analysis. Others discover best spontaneously, on the run. While a logical sequence runs from chapter one to chapter five, you may choose to read the book in a different order. You can read it quickly or slowly, front to back, in one or two sittings or in small chunks on a bus, park bench or abandoned log on a dry river bed. From time to time, you can also take a relaxing breath, flip it open and read what presents itself. Regardless of your approach, the best way to bring your full consciousness to the pieces is to reflect on your life experience as you read. This includes paying attention to the passages that move your emotions.

As you read, or when you finish as much of the book as you want to read, you can go straight to the goodies, choosing to act or reflect on what has the most relevance to you right now. You can start with a few doable themes that allow you to gain some quick victories. Or you can begin by tackling a monster issue. This will probably work best if you either 1) get up and do it immediately or 2) slot it into your schedule as you would with any other important task.

You may feel that some parts of the book have no immediate relevance to you. Take a second look. They could be the most important sections of all. If this turns out not to be the case, don't read them. Putting the book on the shelf and re-visiting from time to time may bring new insights in light of your ongoing experience. But when it runs out of juice, and if it fails to hold sentimental value for you, it may be time to give it away or sell it. In this way, the old soldier can obtain a new lease on life in someone else's hands.

Your authority comes from honouring your own experience in discovering who you really are and what you are here to do. This is all the authenticity you need. Your life is your practice and that is drama enough. I hope the book helps you to reduce the instances where you feel you must choose the lesser of evils and to increase the occasions where you can choose what is best for you, the people you love and the world around you.

CHAPTER ONE

STEP BACK AND SEE THE BARS ON THE CAGE

"Let us not look back in anger or forward in fear but around in awareness"

James Thurber

1. Listen to the Canaries

Neil Postman's foreword to his provocative book, *Amusing Ourselves to Death*, features an interesting comparison between the prophetic writings of George Orwell (*1984*) and Aldous Huxley (*Brave New World*).[1] While they are widely assumed to have foretold the same things, Postman draws a sharp contrast between them.

Orwell feared that we would have oppression imposed upon us, with the state, Big Brother, turning us into a captive culture. Huxley warned that our love of new technologies and other comforts would undermine our capacity to think and that we would preoccupy ourselves with brief, shallow pleasures.

Orwell predicted that we would be controlled by the inflicting of pain and destroyed by forces that we hate. Huxley believed we would be controlled through the inflicting of pleasure and destroyed by the things that we love.

Orwell feared those who would ban books. Huxley was afraid that no one would want to read them.

What do you think?

It may be tempting to say that only the lives of the troubled, such as drug-dependent people, relate to Huxley's observations. After all, instant gratification, ignoring of consequences and increasing self-absorption are at the heart of drug-dependent behaviour.

But people do not develop drug-related problems in a vacuum and drug-dependent people are not a class apart from the rest of us. Their preoccupations and problems reflect those of the society around them. We live together in a society soaked in Huxley's concerns, a society obsessed with material wealth, new technologies, famous people, artificial excitement - and forgetful of those left behind.

Mining companies used to determine if the air could support life in the work environment by placing a canary into a cage and lowering it into the mine. If the canary died, the miners would not enter their own cages into the workplace. Drug dependency, the poverty and homelessness fostered by the huge gap in income between richest and poorest, obsession with empty-calorie information and devotion to instant gratification and violence-as-entertainment are just some of our society's canaries. They warn us that the times and places we live in do not sustain life as well as they should.

If we step back far enough we can gain greater insight into how this drama unfolds and how it drains our energies every day.

2. Step Back and See the Bars On the Cage

Each of us participates in a kind of hallucination that assures us of tranquility and a place in the sun if we simply figure out society's rules and follow them. I suggest that there's some exaggeration in the notion of wisdom that embraces us when we strive to follow the tribe's rules without reservation. My permanent itch insists it's a room filled with smoke and mirrors.

The fast pace of life is only part of it. We float in a sea of permanent noise that promises fulfillment around the next corner but rarely delivers what we need. Like the kid who goes to the carnival seeking the sensual delight promised by the carnival barker, we often enter the tent and get rolled. Being increasingly needy, we save our money and come back for more stimulation and pain.

We do not completely volunteer for this dead-end cycle. It's just that the carnival can overwhelm our senses. We cannot be free of the hustle until we step back and observe the true nature of the noise. Here are some of its forms.

Speed

Speed is our predominant religion. It soaks through our lives absolutely so that we unthinkingly accept it as a law of nature and consume our best energies struggling to catch up, keep up and avoid falling farther behind. I remember the days when newspapers, magazines, books and television programs warned of the approaching crisis in filling the gobs of time we would have at our disposal as a consequence of time-saving technology. We have since discovered that computers, fax machines, cell phones, express mail and microwaves have " liberated " us to run a perpetual race to everywhere and nowhere.

A lot of us feel that we choose busy-ness. It's like watching television with a remote control. In a matter of seconds we can see the news, a quiz show, a basketball game, *The Three Stooges on Mars*, weather highlights, a city council meeting, a *Green Acres* rerun and a commercial for shampoo that produces orgasms. But we will not see a complete program. Instead, we will be exposed to bite-sized chunks of nothing lacking any connection to each other or to some unifying entity.

We are continuously faster at moving faster, more organized in meeting the day's urgencies and racing toward a future that belongs to somebody else. The busier we are the more important we feel. Chasing and catching goals allows us to belong in the race with others. Productivity means self-worth. Idleness used to be a status symbol. Now, having no time confers status.

Speed is also propelled by fear of boredom, being ignored, dying. If we keep moving we keep isolation and loneliness a step behind. But the sprint to fill our lives with possessions and stimulations deprives us of the ability to feel and see what nourishes our silent cores, the essence of us. While we take comfort where we can, we become less joyful, less patient, less spontaneous and less able to enjoy the present. Lonely for ourselves, we can find it difficult to resist being pulled into a Las Vegas world of artificial shine and non-stop action, in which we retreat toward the attention span of three-year-old toddlers.

Traditional time management does not help us to counteract our domination by speed because it is a tool of speed. It is an agent of the machine. It says there is never enough time and never will be. It shows us how to cram more into less time rather than shift our rhythms so that we conduct our lives in ways that include fun and that which we value most.

According to the rules of traditional time management, to say that slower is beautiful is to risk being seen as a slacker out of touch with the times. To insist that journeys are far more important to us than departures and arrivals invites condescension. In this environment, even leisure activities demand urgency. Speed's challenge to keep up is a shell game that keeps us too preoccupied to notice the other bars on the cage.

Information

We are overwhelmed by the useless information we swallow every day. It comes to us through limitless channels and we are conditioned to receiving it and chasing it, as if getting more information of any kind will help us cope with the anxiety and emptiness we too often feel. According to Kalle Lasn and Bruce Grierson, we are at a loss for how to respond to it:

> *"We can't sweat it out, or excrete it, or trash it. It stays, imperfectly stored, somewhere, taking up space, forever. The result is a low-level tension, as if we're perpetually preparing for an exam that never comes. As if we've been sent out to gather branches in the woods; we pick up everything and put down nothing until we buckle under the weight of the impossible load."* [2]

Our technological environment seems limitless in the diversions and information it offers. The internet provides a cosmos of information both useful and useless. The more of it we read and hear, the less we know because we see less of the real world where it originates.

Television puts a telescope to the latest developments in the lives of people who glitter. Tabloids lie about prominent people and inform us that a half-fish, half-human has washed up on the California coast (with pictures). Glossy magazines track the careers of celebrities on the rise, at the peak and on the skids. We are literally under assault by empty-calorie information that requires nothing of us beyond titillation and purchase.

We lack the sense of any emerging big picture because the information comes to us in fragments lacking continuity. At the same time, we are less and less anchored in the feeling of who we are, uncertain about what our true relationship with the world should be. We have become too concerned about our roles and functions in life and too remote from our dreams.

To turn information, knowledge and life's challenges into wisdom we need to experience purpose and fun in our daily lives. Being in touch with our values and aspirations helps us to emerge from the cyclone of our predatory times and enter a more harmonious flow. We can't do that while chasing or being pulled by the short-term escapes of technological toys and information volcanoes.

Modern Economics

The corporate economy that dominates the globe stimulates investment and business diversity as well as employment that enables some people to take care of their basic needs and others to achieve a comfortable lifestyle. In *The Turning Point*, Fritjof Capra points out the limited perspective of this system:

> *"Economists generally fail to recognize that the economy is merely one aspect of a whole ecological and social fabric; a living system composed of human beings in continual interaction with one another and with their natural resources, most of which are, in turn, living organisms."* [3]

In our system, important economic decisions are often made without consideration of their consequences for people and other living things. Destruction and slaughter stimulate economic growth. The hugely successful marketing of cigarettes took no account of their disastrous consequences to health. Tobacco companies suppressed for many years research that exposed these effects. And the costs of treating sick and dying users is included in the gross national product, a measure of economic health. The demise of croplands, forests, the creatures of the air, land and water, and the tenant cultures that they support, further demonstrates the side effects when profit seeking has no limits.

As privileged world citizens, global corporations have a free ride so long as they make big profits and keep growing. They do not compete so much as form alliances in order to exploit common opportunities wherever in the world they might exist. They can live where they want to and, like gigantic amoebae, change shape at will by selling pieces of themselves, acquiring other companies and ejecting a few hundred or a few thousand employees. They control most of the world's flow of information and news.

Global corporations are often separate from civil society rather than integrated and accountable parts of it. In fact, they have become the centre of gravity, dominating civil society, where our basic humanity is supposed to be channeled through the exercise of citizen responsibility, compassion, trust and the struggle to treat each other as equals. The more dominant they become, the less they seem to honour values outside of their own. Many of them develop interest in correcting industrial pollution, crime, violence and human rights only when investments are threatened.

Citizens of civil society have become disposable consumer units in the global corporate reality. By definition, if we lack money or credit we do not exist unless we get some money or credit. If we have a lot of money to spend we are more valued corporate citizens than people with average amounts of money to spend or little money to spend. In order to maintain our membership in the firm we must spend our money or obtain credit.

Advertising is inescapable, seducing and ridiculing us into acquiring what it insists we need, deserve and must obtain simply because we are able to. The definition of need has shifted. Necessity has become whatever we can get. We cannot do without anything. We constantly acquire therefore we exist. When we cease to acquire we cease to exist. Entitlement, accumulation and immediate gratification have been made heroic.

People who live on the street are object lessons to the rest of us living in a society where the social service net is being dismantled. In addition to being scapegoats for our frustrations, they personify the elimination of human beings who will not or cannot belong to the firm. They remind us that they could be us

A Word About Universal Plastic

Global franchises sterilize our environments by ensuring that their outlets in one location look pretty much like their outlets in any other location. The yellow, red and blue plastic buildings along neon commercial strips have replaced the varied architecture and rich textures that flourished in the downtown cores where the hearts of our communities used to beat.

The more time we spend in non-stop artificial environments, the less we feel a sense of place and community. No matter how far or how fast we travel, the same franchise restaurants, strip malls and service stations hypnotize us. Numbed rather than nourished by these candied and homogenized surroundings, we are more likely to seek relief in mass-produced, cookie-cutter products and less likely to appreciate the uniqueness of goods and services provided by local businesses. We are in danger of becoming exiles in our own communities.

Horror

Much of the violence we see in our society is classified as entertainment - as a way to release tensions. But how much relief is there in playing a computer game that gives points for killing the bad guy even if it means slaughtering innocent people in the process? How much relief is there in watching hours and hours of violence in children's cartoons and in prime time? Our sensitivities are not so much relieved as blunted by actual and pretend violence.

Being accessible to virtually all of us, television does the best job of dulling our sense of horror in the face of tragedy. The news presents motion pictures of destruction and death that momentarily shock and mortify us but immediately rescues us from yuckie emotions by featuring ten seconds of blow-dried anchor leading us into a story about a puppy caught up a tree. Then the real agenda unfolds as we are delivered to the advertisers.

In the mass-marketing arena, the greatest sin is refusal to consume products that redeem us. In commercials we learn that gluttony is expected because tablets wash away our sins. Anticipating the pain before a night out, we receive instructions to pop the pills *before* pigging out can produce its logical consequences. Commercials are places of worship which direct us to the fulfillment of our need for acceptance (toothpaste), status (cars), belonging (beer) and sexual attractiveness (space limitations do not permit...).

Tragedy is presented as part of a kaleidoscope of spectacles whose prime purpose is to sell products. Floods, earthquakes and mass death are acts in the ongoing media variety show that delivers us to the holy water of new-and-improved. Tape footage of bombing victims loses its impact on our sense of compassion when it gives way to the grade school choir story that comes just ahead of the beer commercial, deodorant add and promos for the hooker-cops-under-cover dramas of sweeps week.

We are forgetting the sacredness of death to the people who die and to those who love them. The depiction of death in frivolous and vicious computer games or its bundling (between commercials) into statistics of hundreds, thousands and millions of people being displaced, maimed and killed dilutes its impact on us, diminishing our personal interaction with tragedy and violating the web that holds humanity together.

The Need To Belong

Among the first things we learn in life is belonging. As part of a family, school, age group, locality, religion or nation, we learn beliefs and codes that ensure survival through membership and acquiescence. Some rules enhance our individual and social lives – respect for others, obedience to law, loyalty to community, regular brushing and flossing. They become the center of gravity for our lives. Other influences require a closer look.

Important people in our lives may expect that we will drag ourselves through medical school when we would prefer to flourish as teachers, artists or plumbers. In various ways they may expect us to put our frivolous needs on the backburner in favour of more "respectable" pursuits. Sometimes we feel more secure just going along and can end up defining ourselves according to what we think others expect of us. These deals that we make in exchange for comfort and belonging can conflict with fully living our lives and make us more vulnerable to broader rules:

To fit in you must stay busy.

You must develop faster ways to swallow information every day.

Those with the most wealth and fame are the most blessed. If you are left behind, you must worship at the altar of those who succeed.

Always remember that red, yellow and blue buildings are your friends and will always be there for you, no matter where you travel.

Making play out of human slaughter sells product, is good for the economy and takes your mind off your problems.

We can't thrive unless we balance fitting into the world with taking the opportunities it provides to become who we are. This means learning to distance ourselves from those influences that get in the way of our becoming self-directed individuals. Getting into the habit of stopping the world and getting off is a good start.

CHAPTER TWO

STOP THE WORLD AND GET OFF

*"In solitude we give passionate attention to our lives,
to our memories, to the details around us."*

Virginia Woolf

1. What Is Time, Anyway?

I have read a lot about time and I keep going in circles. My dictionary defines it as " the physical quantity measured by clocks, " then spends eight column inches looking at it through various telescopes. As a result, I suspect but cannot prove that it is a parlour trick being played on us all. But let me be pragmatic. Since we cannot afford to sit back and do nothing all the time and since we constantly move toward death, I'll say it exists. That way we can distract ourselves from our anxieties for a while.

If we accept that it exists, we have to accept that we cannot gain time, catch up to it or lose it, because it's always there, twenty-four hours every day, seven days every week, through all the years and decades of our lives. No matter what we do. Every bit of it, all the time, filling everything to the brim and beyond. We can spend it like drunken sailors but it never goes away.

So let's throw out the notion of time as something that we lack and recognize that our permanent racing to meet outside demands can cut us off from the time available to do things that we really want to do. Let's also recognize our conditioning to society's insistence that time is a straight-line production rocket that dictates our responsibilities while ignoring our personal needs.

The production model of time serves an important purpose in laying out deadlines, quotas, predictable arrivals, departures, openings and closings. But it fails to recognize our inner experience, insisting that the only real time is outside of us, symbolized on a watch or clock. Production time is a close cousin of leisure time, which is designed to "re-create" us through diversion and self-improvement. During leisure time we go to the gym, take self-improvement courses, read the right magazines, attend school reunions and rush to concerts by eight p.m. These activities whip us into shape for more work.

I mentioned previously that time management is an agent of the machine that keeps us racing. Watches and clocks are instruments of time management. Our relationship with timepieces can trap us and make us forget the real origins of the pressure. A digital watch presents one set of numbers reflecting the current instant. It reminds us of its absolute authority and that, *right now*, we need to get to a meeting, deliver a package, squeeze in some exercise, catch an airplane. It conditions us to feel rushed and exhausted, assuring us that important people have no time.

A dial watch allows us to see where we have been, where we are now and where we are headed. But instead of making us more conscious of time's eternity, it convinces us that we have none, helping us to envision a forbidding future if we should fail to meet demands on time. In these ways, watches and clocks feed the economy, which depends upon us being permanently anxious about the future and looking for relief.

Supporting and feeding our efforts to catch up, the marketplace responds by selling us fast food, fast cars, faster computers and time management books that train us to squeeze more and more activity into less and less time. It also recognizes that we will occasionally reflect on the past, feel regret at what we left behind and be vulnerable to appropriate nostalgia products and getaways at low, low prices.

The marketplace equips our fantasies and nostalgia by providing clothing designed to wrap us in 60's radicalism without the risk, 70's escapism with an ironic grin and 80's wealth without the wealth. It relieves our longing for the primitive and mystical with Peruvian rugs, ceramic gods and Mexican serapes. To ensure our continuing comfort in unfamiliar surroundings it makes franchise hamburgers available in locations adjacent to the ancient Egyptian and Central American pyramids. And, for those of us lacking the stomach to actually go into the wilds, there are antiseptic spa weekends clothed in flannel shirts, stonewashed jeans and $300 hiking boots that need never see a trail or a hill.

Our expectations, fears and recollections ensure that the future and the past become more real to us than the present. Despite the fact that we have no chance of experiencing the real world unless we live in the present, we have no time for it. We console ourselves that one day we will catch up to the future and clear up the past.

As the greyhounds in the race, we can never catch the mechanical rabbit unless the system that propels it breaks down. Actually, this would have its good points. The realization and acceptance that the rabbit is an illusion designed to make us run could set us free. But until the day we find ways to opt out of the race or run it at our own speed we will not truly inhabit ourselves or the world around us.

The good news is that the race is smoke and mirrors and there's enormous potential for freeing ourselves. This requires that we manage our time effectively, which really means managing ourselves effectively. We are the designers of our time consumption, as we are the designers of our space consumption. We cannot make our watches decelerate time but we can change the rhythm and direction of our dance with it. We can make watches servants rather than dictators...and give them regular time off.

Traveling harmoniously through time is like navigating long-distance on a river or an ocean, where the shortest distance between two points is rarely a straight line. Long-distance navigation involves complicated calculations influenced by the seasons and the earth's rotation. A voyage from point A to point B requires attention to many factors, including the effects of shifting winds, changing water currents, convergence of weather systems, avoidance of other craft on shipping lanes and the need to sail around or ride storms. The route is circuitous, the voyage prompts fear as well as euphoria, and both well-being and successful arrival depend on the marriage of uncontrollable forces and the navigator's skills.

Accepting our role as navigator means recognizing the difference between what we can and cannot control. Among our skills as navigators is the care and feeding of our personal rhythms, which live in relationship with the rhythms outside of us. Personal time enables us to take care of ourselves through solitary contemplation and being with people because we want to. It allows us to walk away, wander aimlessly, play, dance and make it up as we go along. It means we breathe freely, lose track of time and replace urgency with passionate involvement in things that we love. And it gives us the space and energy to pause and be fully present to the beauty in a sunset, the wind in the trees, the ripples in a lake or a child at play – to be conscious of these and more ordinary things as if for the first time.

It is unconditional. It justifies itself. It does not require a watch.

Here's a suggestion for putting time in its proper place. Take off your watch and put it somewhere out of sight that is not your pocket. Spend at least two hours without it, doing what you normally do if you enjoy it, or switching to something that you would rather do. Try to make it an activity you enjoy so much that it lets you lose track of time for a while. This could be a work task or it might mean doing nothing, going for a walk, visiting a friend, hitting a bucket of golf balls or buying that new pair of space sneakers. Postpone any production-time appointments that get in the way.

Create time blocks away from the watch every day - for regular, sustained periods or more frequently, for shorter durations. During these times, let enjoyment dictate your rhythms. When we watch time going by in numbers, we forget to live fully. In order to remember, we have to feel ourselves living the process.

2. Live In the Hurricane's Eye

I'm sitting in a sun chair near our cabin on a northwest shore of Lake Peninsula, near Huntsville. My wife Lynda and I decided to follow up Toronto's glitter and noise with the peace and natural solitude of Cedar Grove Lodge and its surroundings. It takes a while but I finally identify and welcome something I have not heard in a long time. Silence.

Talk about beautiful clichés. A loon floats by and the lake under it is a mirror reflecting the technicolour forest on the opposite autumn shore. The double vision is a conspiracy involving the lake, the forest and God - a show-biz attempt to jolt me away from the world's noise so that I can marvel at what's staring back at me. It works.

Serenity goes beyond relaxation and brings us to a state of mind where we become re-acquainted with the things we've forgotten – the smell of bush green, the uniqueness of people we know – the rhythm and joy of following a good baseball game pitch by pitch.

You didn't think I'd leave out baseball did you?

Anyway, it's not easy to become serene. We first have to remove the coat of daily noises that promotes fear of the future, regret of the past and forgetfulness about who we really are inside. Noise is a modern drug that affects all of our senses. It has many forms – sounds that interfere with our rhythms, junk mail, pollution, people who drain our energies, injustice, disabling fear. The list is long.

The crazy thing is we get used to it and silence gets scary. We even hesitate to spend time alone with ourselves.

In order to kick this drug we have to go through withdrawal. The hard part is learning to live without it even though it seems to be everywhere. In order to be in touch with ourselves and the miraculous beauty that surrounds us, we have to learn to be in the noise but not of it — to live in the calm eye of the hurricane where we can move toward relaxation and arrive at serenity.

Later that morning the wind picks up and the water starts slapping the shore. But it's not noise. It's music.

3. Be Like Water

Life is more about dynamic fluctuation than static balance. Every day we go through inescapable cycles of sorrow and joy, solitude and relationship, confidence and self-doubt, accomplishment and failure. Our natural rhythms want and need to flow among these and other extremes. Consciously accepting the truth of this dance as our natural condition can reduce unrealistic expectations and free us to be more accepting of our voyages in the world.

Have you ever noticed that water never gets in its own way? It doesn't need to be fierce to get the job done. We can have our tensions drained and senses awakened by a quiet lake or by exploding rapids that engulf us in cleansing spray smelling vaguely of wet leaves. Living our lives embodies the dynamics of water – acting without forcing, according to our natural rhythms.

Being like water is a form of conscious living that lets us get out of our own way and live fully. It means investing less energy in dealing with life's problems. Rather than promoting laziness, however, conscious living teaches us the intelligent use of energy. Reducing wasted effort actually increases the energy we have available to invest in what has importance for us.

We can't always get to lakes, rivers or oceans. And it's a major stretch for most of us to retreat to monasteries beside mountain streams in order to meditate and receive instruction from ancient sages. But we can free up our own waters in countless ways every day.

We can start by looking directly at reality, seeing it for ourselves without techniques, fears or someone else's beliefs. If we can accept what we see without judgement, we put ourselves in position to slow down and respond from our hearts and intuition, where much of life is supposed to be lived.

Constantly rushing and forcing makes us fearful and buries our natural ability to make good decisions. When we trust our intuitive ability to immediately see what is significant and balance it with our ability to think, we can gradually step back and deliberately make outside pressures wait in line for attention. This is consistent with what Taoists call the art of *wu-wei* – of swimming with the current, acting with the grain and waiting for the right moment.

Living in this way means acting confidently and spontaneously, unburdened by fear of failure and concern for status. It enables us to differentiate real from imagined dangers and to see our surroundings with less anxiety and more clarity. And it changes our relationship with time so that it becomes friend rather than enemy, servant rather than master.

4. Be Fully Present

I once watched a documentary on Mother Teresa of Calcutta in which, at the height of civil warfare in Beirut, Lebanon during 1982, she was shown negotiating with United Nations officials in an attempt to obtain permission to enter West Beirut and escort to safety the people under siege there. Mother Teresa insisted on going in during the fighting but officials would agree to grant permission only after the declaration of a legitimate cease-fire.

During the debate an official inquired as to how she would propose to get the people out during the fighting. "One at a time", she replied." "You see, I always feel like this…if I didn't pick up the first person, I would have never picked up 42,000 in Calcutta from the streets. So, I think, one at a time."

Mother Teresa's one-pointed focus should not be mistaken for naïve commitment to doing Christ's work. Rather, it reflects *mindful* commitment to doing Christ's work. In these negotiations she considered the needs of the people in danger, the perilous situation that confronted her, the agenda of the officials, her influence and tactics, the capabilities of her organization and her own spiritual mission. Her total grasp of the big picture informed her single-minded determination.

As with Mother Teresa, so with the rest of us. " One at a time " can revolutionize our lives. It means being totally present and committed – in complete contact with ourselves and our environment without leaking energy and awareness to fear and other limitations. This state of awareness may last for short periods but leaves a legacy to build on. It makes us observers, able to detach from distracting thoughts while fully accepting ourselves and the situation in which we happen to be living.

This ability to step outside of distractions, even for a short time, allows us to cultivate a kind of internal compass that provides stability and direction in our constantly-changing relationship with life. Zen Master Shunryu Suzuki once illustrated this point by suggesting that, to fully appreciate the sights we see from a train, we need to avoid looking only at the tracks because it will prevent us from seeing the sights and also make us dizzy. [1]

Stepping back from the close-up details and self-absorptions of our lives and relaxing into a simple awareness of what's outside and inside of us, frees up the natural intelligence that allows us to keep flowing between soft focus on the big picture and hard focus on what lies six inches in front of our faces. As a result, we force less and deal more creatively with the task at hand according to a deeper sense of what is appropriate.

It's like reading, where we ordinarily pay complete attention to the words and meaning of what is being read. By stepping back, we can gain a greater appreciation of the book itself, of its composition – pages, printed words, ink, fabric of the paper, durability or flexibility of the cover and overall beauty. By stepping back even farther, we can gain an understanding of the book's larger meaning by learning something about the author's life and views, and the era in which the book was written. And we can learn about ourselves by reflecting upon where the book has touched us. With this awareness we build a greater understanding of the book's real meaning for the author and for us. Here are three ideas for being fully present:

1. Take time to live life deliberately. Give your complete attention to what you are doing, as if it is the only thing. Leave thoughts of the past and the future out of it. Go easy on yourself by detaching from thoughts of how you and other people ought to be. Accept the validity of your own and others' experience. Each of us walks a different path but we wander in the same forest, trying to find our way.

2. Learn to live with uncertainty. Be open to seeing events, people and surroundings without rushing to analyze and summarize with pre-cooked formulas that give you a feeling of familiarity but limit the opportunity for new insights. As often as possible, move from mental to physical activity and let solutions to problems come to you there.

3. Get to know yourself. Observe your responses to your experiences. Get used to noticing when you feel joy, anxiety, anger and serenity. Notice how you breathe, move and gesture under the influence of different emotions. Do not judge what you see - just observe. Listen to your body's need for rest and relaxation. Treat yourself the way you want others to treat you.

We live fully in the present when we have stepped out of our own way and achieved calmness and clarity. We recognize the truth only in the present. In this life, that is the closest we come to eternity.

5. Give Beauty the Time and Attention It Needs

Finding beauty is impossible when our energy and concentration is drained by speed and anxiety. That's when we overlook the extraordinary in the ordinary. Beauty flourishes when we accept the truth that everything has importance, including what we happen to be doing at any given time. We create beauty when we are mindful of our process rather than obsessed with its outcome

Mindfulness is nothing more nor less than awareness without judgement, fear or preconception, where we step outside of our obsessions and see things as they are, with our whole mind. This works best without the interference of techniques or obedience to high dogma. It boils down to making ourselves totally available right now.

Natural surroundings promote mindfulness. Trees tell me whether or not I'm centered. They relax and energize me. My gnat's attention span expands in their presence. Trees in winter and summer tend to catch my attention first. I notice them as soon as I look out the window or walk out the door. When I snowshoe or walk in the bush, they conspire with the wind and talk to me. I touch some of them and talk back.

But when I chase deadlines or chop myself into pieces through impatience and a tendency to speed, the trees exist only as a vague backdrop to my immediate melodramas. They seem to be located in a different world. In fact, they *are* located in a different world – the real world.

I used to go months rushing through my parallel universe, calling time-out only when I became ill, depressed or bound up in a work crisis. Gradually, I've learned to pay attention to early symptoms which include alienation from the trees, the wind, the birds and the four-leggeds. Under these conditions, walking away from the noise and into natural surroundings goes to the top of the agenda. The transition time keeps getting shorter.

Trees dance with the eternal energy of life, absorbing what's around them, bending with the extremes of climate, dancing with the wind, filtering the unseen and giving clean air to the rest of us. They live redemption every day and re-enter the earth when they are very old and very dry, having given all they have to give on the surface. They speak to people who grieve, fear and despair, teaching us that the downtimes have beauty too, healing us for the inevitable return to new beginnings and growth.

But we can enjoy beauty without hugging trees. We can create beauty in our relationship with our surroundings and activities. The only requirement is that we remove the blinders and allow ourselves the freedom to relate fully to everyday things. The opportunities continuously present themselves:

1. Start the morning by letting yourself slowly wake up for at least a half hour. Feel the self-indulgence of your body as it basks in the calm of sleep hangover. Don't get in the way. Listen to the sounds outside and smell breakfast cooking. Let your body stretch when it wants to and let it dictate your breathing. Get up slowly and follow where your body wants to go. Probably to the bathroom but you get the idea. Rather than confining this to statutory holidays and weekends, try to do it every day.

2. Let yourself laugh from the belly when something funny happens.

3. Watch how the shadows outside shift as the day progresses, feel the differences in how you perceive your surroundings and notice how the daily routines of people and animals relate to the changing light.

4. Listen to the sound of vehicle traffic until you discern a rhythm.

5. *Eat a banana just to eat a banana*, rather than to get your daily quota of potassium. Smell it before and after you peel it. Chew each piece slowly and feel the texture of the fruit. Notice the taste. Allow yourself to feel grateful for the nourishment and the experience.

The old saying about beauty being in the eye of the beholder does not go far enough. Beauty exists everywhere all the time, whether we behold it or not. And we always have the choice of opening ourselves to it in all that we see, feel and do.

6. Digest Your Experience

It all depends on your point of view.

A snail is plodding down the street when two turtles slowly make their way out of an alley and gradually approach him. When they finally arrive, they proceed to beat him to a pulp. It takes them a couple of hours and when they finally finish punching, pinching and kicking the snail, the turtles spend another hour turning him onto his shell, upside down. They leave him torn, swollen and bleeding and move down the street inch by inch before slowly disappearing around a corner.

The snail rocks himself back and forth for two hours and finally roles over on his stomach. He waddles painfully down the street until he arrives at the closest police station. It takes him another hour to climb the steps and enter the door. Upon seeing him the desk sergeant is horrified. " Good heavens, snail! You look *terrible*! What *happened* to you? "

" I don't know, " says the snail. " It all went by so fast! "

Each of us is unique and views life through a different telescope. A crisis for one person means a joyride for someone else. An hour can be eternal for some of us, an eye-blink for others. But we have a fundamental need in common. In order to nourish our uniqueness, each of us requires space and time for reflection. If he's to get his life back on track, even the snail will need to retreat and reflect.

When we reflect we turn down the volume of uncontrolled thinking and action-for-action's-sake, pausing so that we can listen to our inner voice, the one that comes from a deeper place. Reflecting means being still so that creative ideas and alternate paths can come to us. If we are fragmented and lacking confidence, reflection can help us to see where we lost our way and to remember what once let us feel sure of ourselves. It can allow us to step back, fully absorb our situation and decide whether it's time to advance, retreat or do more preparation.

When we give ourselves time to reflect, we increase our chances of seeing the difference between our true aspirations and some of the demands being thrown at us. We are more likely to examine all sides of an issue and arrive at long-term solutions rather than band-aid remedies that create their own sets of new problems. We give ourselves the space to assess the motivations of experts and advisors, and distinguish between good and bad advice. Reflection provides the opportunity to notice good ideas that, in our haste, we may have overlooked. And it can help us notice where our relationships need strengthening.

One of the casualties of our speed-oriented lifestyle is the time to acknowledge our own passages in life. Digesting our experience enables us to step back and see our accomplishments - the milestones on our journeys. It lets us know when success in raising the money for the new playground signals a time to celebrate or buy ourselves something frilly. Monitoring the good stuff reminds us to live the joy of the trip and makes it easier to notice the helpful coincidences and gifts of the universe that stare at us every day but are often obscured by our addiction to worry.

In addition to space and time, reflection requires commitment from us. And while the space is usually available on a park bench, in a library or at a cottage by a lake, our homes can provide the handiest times and places for reflection. Here are a couple of ideas for cultivating space and time for reflection in your life:

Create Your Own Space. A sanctuary is a place of renewal that can help you increase your sense of freedom. Whether an office or converted corner, it works best when you control whether others can interrupt you. You can customize it to your needs and style. And it can evolve over time, with you.

In this space you can keep some of your favourite books, tapes, talismans and smelly sneakers. You can organize your stuff, put up strange pictures and post inspirational poems. You can surround yourself with candles, stones and a dream-catcher or two. A desktop that is not used for information storage holds fewer distractions and makes it easier to empty mental baggage. You may or may not want a window to the outside. Located off the basement rec room, my office, a converted bedroom, looks out on a major highway for neighbourhood cats who stop regularly to say hi and successfully solicit treats.

In the privacy of your space, you call the shots. Write journal entries, plan and review your day, pray, stare at the wall, celebrate the silence, light some candles, pig out on chocolate, plot your next moves, build scale models, listen to music, read spiritual books, consolidate ideas or just dream. You can eliminate any useless tasks from your agenda that interfere with your self-indulgence. And you can do all this at *your* speed, not the world's.

It may be difficult to decide that you will create the space. Acquiring the territory may require both diplomacy and firmness with loved ones. And you may need a transitional period to get used to it. But you will know you have arrived when, upon entering it, you begin to feel grounded at the prospect of downtime alone.

Begin and end the day with yourself. When you get up each morning spend at least twenty minutes in your space. Try to set up occasional days when you can allow yourself an extra hour or three if you need them. If you commit daily to the twenty minutes, you also condition yourself to expansion that can support your evolving needs.

Own this time and use it to relax and determine what your day will be about. It's up to you. Drink coffee, let your mind wander, meditate, do warm-up exercises, stare at the surroundings, read something to energize, relax and focus you. Then demand that priorities for the day earn their way onto your agenda. Leave some empty space in your schedule for the unexpected and your own shifts in direction.

Invest a few minutes at night being still, reflecting on the day and getting organized. Draft a short list of tasks and appointments for the next day but do not give them official status until next morning. Let your deeper intelligence screen them overnight so that you can identify and approve only the essential items next morning.

Establishing space and time to consider the direction of our lives may seem unrealistic in view of daily pressures to run full-out and postpone the luxury of renewal and self-care until more idyllic times - like retirement. But the point of reflection time is timeless - to pause long enough to renew ourselves and increase the creativity of our decision-making so that our investment of time and energy strikes a healthy balance between what the heart wants and what the world demands.

7. Breathe

It's easy to appreciate the important role that breathing plays in our lives. We just need to reflect on our experience. Look around. Its absence makes the heart grow still. People without it grow pale and stop moving. Without it we feel as if time takes forever. Let's face it, breathing enables everything to happen, if we let it. My name is Dennis and I'm a lousy breather. This is my story.

I have tried breathing to reduce stress. I have tried breathing to slow down a pounding heart. I have tried breathing to clean out my lungs. I have tried breathing designed to bring me insight. I've even tried breathing aimed at transcendence.

Yes, sisters and brothers, I've counted breath, smiled while breathing, half-smiled while breathing, measured breath by footsteps, breathed shallow and breathed deep. I'm no damn good at any of it. In fact, breathing has been one of my weaknesses for as long as I can remember.

I once drove home on a desolate highway for three hours following a day-long meeting which turned out to be one more in a long series of stressful events during that deadening cycle of my life. About halfway home, tingling, followed by numbness and tightness, made their way up my fingers, hands and arms. I began to have difficulty breathing and felt as if I was going to lose consciousness. My hands locked and I could barely move my fingers.

I pulled over and walked along the highway, looking for relief from fresh air and a little exercise. It seemed to help but when I resumed driving, the numbness and tightness returned. Insisting this was not a stroke, I floored the pedal toward the next restaurant and a phone. When I entered the restaurant I felt slightly better so I ate a sandwich, phoned the Ontario Provincial Police, told them who and where I was, gave them my home telephone number and address, and asked them to look for me if I hadn't called them from home in two hours. Deep-breathing into a plastic bag, I made it home, informed the police and crawled humbly into bed.

After several more of these episodes, I realized that I was hyperventilating as part of a reaction to stress that included chest pains, ulcers, depression and runaway anxiety. I gradually learned to recognize occasions when anxiety and anger produced rapid, shallow and irregular breathing, shortness of breath, throat clearing, muscular tension, hunched posture and runaway heart rate. With the twin realizations of my emotional state's dramatic influence on my breathing and vice-versa, I finally accepted that I had been a tense and shallow breather for most of my life. I was going to have to learn how to breathe.

I approached the new era of breathing in ways that had created the stress in the first place. I set a list of goals and began to learn as many breathing techniques for cleansing, tranquilizing and transcending as I could find in books, videos and workshops. Breathing became yet another in a groaning list of priorities. As it turns out, I possessed neither the time nor the energy to follow through. My jagged breathing continued and I felt a sense of growing frustration and failure. But my continuing health problems finally bludgeoned me into a state of surrender – the acceptance that total mastery of all the techniques was beyond my capabilities and needs.

Once I accepted the sheer zaniness of trying to develop breathing skills for all occasions, it was a short hop to seeing that I simply needed to let my body breathe the way it wants to breathe. I began to set aside more " walk away " time where I could relax and learn to get out of my own way. I came to see that laughter and exercise released the tension and that feelings of joy and absorption in beauty brought smooth breathing, improved posture and regular heartbeat.

Although I don't levitate yet, I'm much better at following my breath rather than leading it. I allow my diaphragm to descend and my abdomen to rise. I witness this without interfering. I do it sitting, standing and lying on the floor. I do it in line-ups, waiting for elevators, watching television, driving the car, walking down the street. When I relapse into shallow speed-breathing, I start over.

In getting out of the way so my body can breathe the way it wants to, I have naturally gravitated to a few practices that have helped me take better care of myself. Most days I boost energy and alertness by increasing the oxygen in my blood stream through ten repetitions of inhaling with mouth closed until my stomach extends about an inch and exhaling with mouth open until stomach goes down to an inch below normal. For quicker uptake I sometimes keep the mouth closed during in- and out-breath. It made me slightly dizzy when I started but my system adapted.

I find the corpse pose relaxing. Simple, and taking only a few minutes, it requires very little of my shallow supply of discipline and patience. I lie on my back on a carpeted floor with my eyes closed. My arms are extended at about 45 degrees and I ground myself by allowing my palms to relax and lie facing the floor. My feet are a couple of feet apart and I let all the body's muscles relax.

I take about twenty gentle and deep breaths from the diaphragm, lasting about five seconds on the in-breath and about seven seconds on the out-breath. Most often my mouth is open but I sometimes inhale through the nose and exhale through the mouth, paying quiet attention to the feel of the breath and the relaxed response of various body parts. I permit intruding thoughts to drift away without fighting them and return to awareness of the breath.

At other times, intense movement frees up the breath and restores it to its natural state. I cycle, run, climb, play basketball, walk and do physical work that, in addition to contributing to fitness, helps keep me from frying in my own wayward juices. My inadequate efforts to learn Tai Chi require that I breathe correctly.

I would like to get to the point where I sit for twenty minutes of meditation twice a day. But the closest I come to sitting meditation happens when, for short periods, I just sit with eyes closed or gaze at water, a tree, a candle flame or the ground. I watch my breath and observe what is happening without forcing. This includes any thoughts that pass through my mind. I let them come and go without judging, while remaining aware of my breathing. The most difficult part is the beginning, when my chattering mind rules. But if I hang in long enough the chattering goes away and I start to notice objects, patterns and connections that have been staring at me since long before I came out of my head to play.

Getting out of the way and giving breath a chance to do the driving lets me drop the exhausting role of controller and go along as a relaxed passenger. This not only helps quiet my mind, it also slows and stabilizes my body's rhythm and I have an easier time letting experiences, thoughts and feelings follow their own course. I become more conscious of my body's need for rest or exercise. I am even less self-conscious with other people.

Not exactly Zen master. But a long way from plastic bags.

8. Be Idle

One of the best ways to restore order in ourselves involves the simple act of walking away from what overwhelms us. Getting better at making outside demands wait means we improve the balance between living from the inside out and living from the outside in. While work enables us to express ourselves and help others, we may forget that the income we receive from it should enhance our freedom to be simply and unconditionally ourselves – in solitude and in communion with other living things.

Idleness and recreation, both important, are not necessarily the same. Recreation refers to activities that we undertake for a purpose; for example, working out at a gym to develop a sculpted body for display or spending a week's vacation on an island in order to re-charge for a return to work. Idleness has no conditions. It is aimless. We freely choose to do anything or nothing for its own sake.

Idleness means we put seriousness to sleep in favour of spontaneity. We permit ourselves the freedom to play in the moment and respond creatively to the unexpected. Dropping our ambitions lets us absorb obvious beauty that is always in front of us but often goes unnoticed – the sudden laughter of a child, the flirtation of a butterfly or the aroma of hamburgers on a grill. As a bonus, our greatest ideas and insights surface when we are not looking.

Some of us are less threatened than others at the prospect of making outside demands wait. But even if the influence of parents, teachers and peers has left us too compliant with others' expectations, we always have the choice of stepping outside of our conditioning. We can determine for ourselves what our pace will be and how we will lose track of time. Here are some ideas.

You can cultivate idleness by declaring a flex day where you simply follow your nose. You can do it any day of the week including Saturday, when many folks work even harder than they do during the rest of the week. This can be scary for workaholics. Try not to have an agenda but if you must, write or type *flex day* where you normally list your tasks and appointments for the day. Beyond that, make no lists and no commitments. That's it. Just make up your day as you go through it.

Don't forget to take off your watch. Tell guilt feelings to wait until tomorrow. When they visit tomorrow ask them where they've been. Let THEM see what it's like. If you genuinely dedicate a day to following your nose, you can be aimless or end up completing chores for fun - getting groceries, mowing the lawn, helping a friend move. Don't think too far ahead. Let whatever you decide originate in the moment and be guided by fun and relaxation.

You can work on a creative project or call time out in a quiet, comfortable place where you let your mind drift, recall a dream and allow deepest thoughts and feelings to surface. You can feed ducks or sit in silence on a bench in the middle of downtown watching people without judging them.

You may want to read a book for fun rather than information. Books are mood-altering drugs that bring peace of mind. Scan a newspaper. Go to a movie. Listen to music that calms or energizes – play air guitar and sing, content in the illusion that you sound as good as the artist in the recording.

Laugh. Dance. Allow yourself to be foolish. Wander aimlessly. See what happens. Collect rocks by a river and build human or animal figures. I'll show you my collection sometime. Take a bike ride because it exhilarates, not because it improves physical fitness or shapes your butt. Try to stay upright while walking some abandoned rails. Come to think of it, I used to do this as a child, announcing to my friends, loudly and dramatically, that I was *The Great Balancio!* Might be time for a comeback.

Visit a sick friend, walk in the rain, renew the habit of hanging out and laughing with family or friends. Take a train ride to a nearby community, have lunch and come back. Climb a hill. Stroll through an unfamiliar neighbourhood.

Learning to be alone is as important as maintaining healthy relationships. In fact, it is an essential building block for developing harmonious relations with all living things. Idleness helps it to happen and we can free it up every day, in brief, ten-minute increments or in day-long escapes. This has nothing to do with self-improvement. It has everything to do with our need to excavate our own rhythms in calm as well as passionate involvement with the things that we love.

CHAPTER THREE

LET GO OF JUNK AND TRAVEL LIGHT

"Stop trying to get organized. When you organize, you're just shuffling the same heavy load. When you simplify, you actually eliminate a large chunk of it. Simplifying is not about doing more in less time. It's about doing less so you'll enjoy it more."

Elaine St. James

1. Die A Little Every Day

I was startled years ago to read the Indian sage Krishnamurti tell an audience that, in order to live fully, we have to die.[1] At the time I had deep doubts about buying into a trip that delivers consolation only in the next dimension. Since then I have stumbled, with increasing relief, toward some understanding of what he meant. In fact, dying every day gives us the freedom to live more completely.

The flow of life consists of one moment that is always passing – a constant process of renewal. Living in the present moment means dancing to this eternal rhythm. We live fully when we create our lives in this series of moments. To do that we have to learn to release whatever gets in the way.

This cycle of death and rebirth exists everywhere and rules the creation of all life. The same forces that produce and constantly renew our skin, blood vessels, nervous systems, thoughts and feelings account for the seemingly accidental events that constantly give birth to leaf patterns, water rapids, mountain ranges, hurricanes, star clusters and galaxies. Everything, including us, is constantly being re-created.

As part of that flow, our experiences expose us every day to opportunities for greater understanding and maturity. These occasions are always with us but we can obscure them with the smoke we create in trying to cope with daily pressures through our attachment to the security of familiar but obsolete beliefs, attitudes and objects.

We all want to feel a sense of purpose, to wake up energized and looking forward to the day. We want to do things right and be stimulated, rather than depleted, by challenges. We desire loving relationships that evolve to new levels. We want to have positive outlooks, feel spiritually grounded and find deeper levels of creativity in ourselves and in our relationship with life.

But we can feel de-valued when we are not preoccupied with racing blindly to keep up with our environment's demands. Its ceaseless blizzards of information can overwhelm us. Communication technology and media unload the world's horrors on us every day. Through sophisticated and insistent marketing, the economic system can lock us into a permanent cycle of easy credit, spending, accumulation, debt repayment and planned obsolescence.

Our rewards for thinking and acting within these boundaries are primarily material. We win prizes, get to eat and drink excessively, buy cars, furniture and grown-up toys at greatly reduced prices. We travel to amusement centres that enable us to pretend that we are children again. We can wind up believing that our reason for being revolves around the accumulation of possessions and sensational experiences. And we can fall into the trap of worshipping these artificial certainties, giving them far more reverence than they deserve.

As consumers, we are constantly called upon to surround ourselves with possessions that deprive us of the space we need to breathe freely. Many of our possessions are like nouns - static objects that just sit there. But it is in our nature to be verbs – the expressers of actions and experiences. Being fully alive means having the freedom to flow as verbs, peeling away the layers of life's mysteries as we go.

Painters and other artists understand this. Paints and brushes record the painter's voyage of discovery, the dance with creative chaos. Novelists' characters take on lives of their own with the writing. Like painters and novelists, we are most alive when we stop worrying about collecting and pigeonholing life and start creating it.

Dying a little every day involves nothing more nor less than detaching from possessions, regrets, self-doubts, behaviours and involvements that smother our ability to absorb the lessons of our experience, so that we increase our awareness of new opportunities. One of the easiest starting points for letting go is also one that most dominates us - the things that we own.

2. Know the Difference Between Junk and Stuff

We can protect and enhance our creative energy by shifting our focus from racing and chasing to pacing and spacing. If we want more time we need to create more space. And vice-versa. The less junk we own the more freedom we have. We can begin by defining for ourselves the difference between junk and stuff.

Junk drains our energies, obscures our spirit and contaminates our judgement by dominating our space, time and attention. We keep cleaning it and moving it, rarely using it. We spend energy serving it that could be invested in higher causes. Junk is a deal with the devil. In exchange for our souls, it protects us from the vulnerabilities of discovering who and why we are.

Stuff has purpose and beauty. It nourishes and energizes us. It's fun and useful, even in storage. It may or may not earn income but it refuses to crowd out other stuff. It allows us breathing space and lets us feel good. And it tells us the truth, providing clues when its time runs out and it approaches junk status.

Junk: A beanie with a propeller that's kept for possible patching material

Stuff: A cheap kite from a popcorn box that has survived two hours in the hands of a laughing, running, screaming, breathless child being called for dinner

Junk: A pile of high-school essays kept for possible review one day

Stuff: A letter from grandmother in 1912, detailing her voyage to the new world

Junk: A jar of bent nails collected between 1952 and 1978

Stuff: Varieties of useable screws spread on tabletops and in containers throughout the house, waiting to be organized

Junk for some of us is stuff for others. That big, overstuffed 1947 armchair with the holes in the upholstery is valued stuff if it brings contentment. Letting go of surrounding junk can give it the space it requires to stand out and add even more value to our lives. Folks who have experienced material deprivation and abuse in arriving at adulthood may take comfort in having possessions that other people may term junk. But it isn't. It's stuff.

Six Reasons Why We Keep Junk

1. It cost a lot of money: The purple Nehru jacket and flowered disco pants purchased during an episode of chemical mood alteration and never worn. A stationary bike found at a yard sale six years ago, dozing and ignored in a corner of the basement.

2. I might need it one day: The cooking element from the wood stove that could be adapted to a gas range. The pants that will come back into style around the same time that their owner loses twenty pounds. The old barbecue brushes, patio stones and used roof shingles that will come in handy during the next depression or world war. Four garbage bags containing 9,187 recipes.

3. It's one of a kind: A butter churner made from dried banana skins. A glove with seven fingers. A petrified hair ball. A candle shaped like Orson Welles.

4. It'll be worth something one day: A jagged piece of Italian marble taken from a house fire. An envelope filled with paper doilies. A bottle of vinegary wine from 1939. A wagon wheel with two spokes.

5. It'll work if I fix it: Six long-playing albums from the 1980's with centres the size of nickels. A home-built 1928 tricycle with iron wheels. A half-scissors waiting for a partner. An eight-track player with mahogany veneer.

6. It was given to me as a gift: A moose lamp from Aunt Ines. A necklace of shark teeth brought back from Florida by Uncle Lester.

The Encyclopedia of Chicken Wings inherited from Grandma Galina. The cracked Porky Pig cookie jar crafted by cousin Kippy Lou.

Material possessions are never neutral. They charge rent and demand attention. They need to be paid for, protected, cleaned, stored, moved repeatedly, shown off and doted on. They demand space, time, emotion and mental energy that could be invested in learning new things, pursuing a dream or doing nothing. Their domination increases over time and they cut us off from the universal flow of life that always invites us to come out and play.

But they also provide a good starting point for clearing our lives of forces that deplete rather than replenish us because they cannot run and they cannot hide. And because some of the rewards of clearing them are immediate, in feelings of lightness and space, moments of inspiration and new appreciation for the possessions that we value.

3. Assess Your Tolerance For Junk

The following 15-point checklist has been designed and scientifically tested so that you can measure your current status as a junk owner. One point for every yes answer, 0 for every no.

1. I have vitamin C capsules from 1983 that have turned to alfalfa.

2. I hang onto old toasters, broken hairdryers and an old zoot suit in case of nuclear war.

3. On nights when the moon is full, the doors and drawers in my home groan.

4. I save old curtain rods, curtains, blinds and mats in case I move into a house where they fit.

5. I own more recipes, cookbooks and maintenance manuals than anybody I know but can't find them.

6. When I lie down to watch T.V. my butt hits the floor and the couch folds around me

7. I have no intention of ever reading two-thirds of the books on my shelves.

8. I'm thinking of patching the holes in my rusted car with my collection of jar lids.

9. There are guests who descended into my basement and have never been seen again.

10. I own 372 screwdrivers and enough paint chips to cover the living room walls.

11. The thought of throwing out jars, broken pens and appointment books from the late 80's leaves me feeling vulnerable to dark forces.

12. I have never seen the top of my desk.

13. I use worn-out socks as elbow pads.

14. I'm thinking of making a sleeping bag out of the lint in the dryer.

15. I have four unused pairs of shoes from the seventies with Cuban heals so high that birds have nested in them.

Score

10+   Terminal condition if continued. You must immediately bring in demolition experts to run controlled fires on half of your possessions.

5-9   Hazardous. You have a tendency to inhale whatever is near you. In a previous life you may have been a goat.

1-4   Normal. If you can call someone who patches rust holes with jar lids normal.

0   Fussbudget. You probably keep your floors so clean that people are afraid to put their feet on them. Ease up and get funky by letting a closet overflow. You spend too much time in the house.

Okay. The rating system has not been scientifically tested. But you know who you are. Suck it up. The following pages will help you to start exorcising the demon of possession.

4. Meet With Yourself

My neighbour Lloyd (not his real name) is a very creative woodworker, mechanic, gardener and handyman who built a double garage to house his wood, tools, tire collection, pipes, bottles and assorted bric-a-brac. He later built an addition onto the garage. There is no room for a vehicle. With the garage full, he erected a structure about half the size of the garage and covered it with tarpaulin. It takes up half the backyard and contains wood. Items can also be found adjacent to each of these structures, the house and the fence.

Some of these possessions enable Lloyd to do interesting and practical things with wood, copper, iron and vegetation. Most of the possessions provide a sense of security to an admirable man who grew up in challenging circumstances. But the possessions cost Lloyd creative time and energy. His most oft-repeated regret is insufficient time to do the many projects that he envisions – time devoted instead to moving and housing his possessions.

The wrestling match between Lloyd's creativity and his possessions mirrors our conflict. On the one hand, desperation or faith may tell us that reducing junk will bring elbowroom and relief. On the other hand, we may feel vulnerable at the thought of releasing some of our props.

We reach an important milestone when we feel any degree of junk fatigue. It means that the pain has surfaced and it's time to go to work. Letting go of obsolete possessions is a lifetime process, as necessary to our well-being as the ruffage in our diet. Here are nine steps for getting started.

1. Meet with yourself. Meeting with yourself can reinforce your intention to de-junk and provide the opportunity to identify some starting points. The first meeting can take place where you feel most comfortable and free from interruption – office, kitchen table, backyard, lake shore, maybe a weekend at a lodge. Your intuition can probably tell you how much meeting time you need - an hour, a half-day, a three-day retreat. Put responsibilities and outside demands on hold. Just giving yourself this time and space is a significant step toward detaching from junk.

2. Consider the big picture. Letting go of possessions may be only one of several areas in your life that you would like to address. Quiet time lets some of these issues surface. Reflecting on your job, relationships, financial situation, health, fitness routine, spirituality and need for solitude can give you clues to other aspects of your life that need attention. Whether we are chaotic pack rats or simple monks, our relationship to our possessions reflects our relationship to other aspects of our lives. You may find that some of these themes will pass through your mind as you clear your possessions. Keep a notebook handy to record these thoughts. Do not ridicule them. They have been waiting for your permission to emerge.

3. Take a tour: Take time out for a preliminary tour - house, garage, car, storage shed, office. Look into drawers, closets, glove compartments, shelves, lockers and boxes. Examine surfaces – tables, desks and floors. In your notebook, list the areas and items that disturb you most or are most easily de-junked.

Get an idea of which items create conflict in your mind and why. This includes the frayed shirts and old magazines that haven't been used in years but stay around because you cannot let go. You can reduce pressure by identifying the easy starting points that will give you momentum and perspective for the more challenging decisions to follow. The experience of the tour and the information you obtain can make the possibilities of de-junking more real in your mind and reinforce your original decision to proceed.

4. Give yourself the time you need. Having some indication of your priorities lets you determine how much cleaning-out time you will require and when that time is best spent. You can pick a season that best matches your rhythms. Winter project? Spring/fall cleaning?

Summer yard sale? You can set aside half days, whole days, successive days, evenings or weekends. Clear your calendar as you would for any other important event.

I've found that adding fifty percent to the original time commitment gives me the space to ride out De-Junk Fever, a mad acceleration that often strikes after the achievement of initial victories. Fuelled by increased momentum and motivation, my eyeballs turn red, an evil leer washes over my face and, steam shooting from my nostrils, I clean out even the most resistant items, slashing and burning my way to new levels of simplicity. Neighbours' complaints about my maniac's laugh in the night fail to stop me.

5. *Think about helpers.* Be careful with this one. A supportive friend or relative can encourage you and help do the physical work. But he/she could also undermine your hard-won resolve by questioning your versions of junk. As it is, you may have to negotiate many choices with a mate and that's challenge enough. You may even have to start by concentrating only on the possessions that are solely yours. Which can be debatable. See what I mean? Screen other people carefully.

6. *Choose the correct clothing for the occasion.* Wear your favourite loose, comfortable clothes, the ones that let you feel most like yourself, that remind you of who you are or who you fantasize yourself to be. Among other things, cleaning out liberates imagination and play because our mental censors get weaker. So feel free to wear the goofy hat and torn jeans that you refuse to throw out but avoid wearing in polite society. They are not junk…they are STUFF!

7. *Choose the appropriate background music.* I prefer rock n' roll, blues, country or Latin music. Favourites include Steve Earle, Lou Reed, Iris DeMent, the Ramones, The Strokes, Emmylou Harris, Santana, Van Morrison, R.L. Burnside and early Elvis, among many others. Engulfed by this background, I dance, sing and occasionally play air guitar. Whatever your preference, you can customize your background to accompany the physical exertion and energy liberation that lie at the heart of cleaning out.

8. Gather your supplies ahead of time. You can always get supplies as you need them but this can interfere with the rhythm you establish as you score small but important victories and build momentum. Gather boxes, garbage bags, labels, post-it notes and a cold water supply. Don't forget the music.

9. Make sure you wear clean underwear. Just kidding. Have a good meal before you start. Include protein but no heavy meats that rob you of energy. No alcohol until the day's work is done. And watch sugar drinks – they'll goose your energy then snatch it away. Cold water is your friend. Did you remember the notebook?

The completion of these nine steps can solidify your motivation and allow you to clarify a starting point. Beyond possessions, the effort you make to complete the preparations will free up awareness and creative thoughts that can guide you in dealing with other obstacles that get in the way of moving toward where you really want and are meant to go.

5. Attack, Divide and Conquer

It took me a long time to stop being a pack rat. My gradual conversion grew out of pain - bruised shins from bumping into obstructions, the deadening repetition of moving things from here to there and back again, and feelings of suffocation. The message finally registered - while they provided breaks from daily pressures, managing possessions consumed time and energy that could be better invested in exploring what my life was really about. The following suggestions come in three phases - attack, divide and conquer. They reflect cooperation with my wife Lynda and imply more order than actually existed at the time.

Attack

1. Take another tour. You may underestimate the extent of the territory where your possessions live (or go to die), especially if your original scan of the territory was brief. Acting on an accurate picture of the extent and location of your possessions reduces the likelihood of discouragement due to surprises that can ambush optimistic expectations. Even the most thorough preliminary examination will fail to uncover all the surprises that can greet you as you progress. So walk the turf again:

Living room/den
Dining room
Kitchen
Laundry
Bedrooms
Bathrooms
Library
Storage shed/areas

Basement
Garage
Car
Attic
Cottage
Office

As you tour these locations, notice the nooks and crannies. In this world, the nooks and crannies have their own nooks and crannies:

Closets
Shelves
Under tables (laundry room included)
Open space beside the furnace
Desk, table and chair surfaces
Medicine cabinets
Refrigerators/freezers
Drawers
Filing cabinets
Trunks

This review can help you to refine your goals and ensure that you have allocated enough time to accomplish the work.

2. Use alternate approaches. You can combine three approaches in attacking junk: location, swiss cheese and category.

The *location approach* concentrates on a particular place that may be the easiest starting point because it contains the most unbearable collection of crap. For example, you may want to start by cleaning out the basement or attic because in those locations the junk most interferes with movement. On the other hand, you may prefer starting in the storage shed because it gets you outside in fresh air and near sunlight.

The *swiss cheese approach* attacks the obvious junk wherever it sits, piles it up and gets it to the dump immediately. This accomplishes short-term victories and a morale boost while increasing space and placing less obvious choices into perspective.

The *category approach* focuses on types of junk regardless of location; for example:

Information – mail, books, magazines, calendars, paper and computer files
Personal effects – wallets, cufflinks, paperweights, key rings
Clothing
Food
Gardening equipment and supplies
Kitchen and laundry equipment and supplies
Entertainment - Music CD's and tapes, videos, DVD's
Unused gifts received from others
Broken stuff – tools, furniture, figurines, lamps, watches
Tabletop knick-knacks

By concentrating on these and other narrow areas the category approach can reduce the scope of each clean-up stage, enabling quick progress that requires smaller time commitments. For example, you could clean out the closets in your home, throwing out or giving away unwanted, unused or fermenting clothes and shoes. You could scan your bookshelves and give away those volumes that you will not read, keep books and articles that you will definitely read and throw out obsolete catalogues, phone books and paper files. In your computer you can clean out useless files and ancient e-mails. And you could gather all the broken stuff in the house and garage, making firm decisions on which watches, lamps, tools and figurines will be repaired and which will be thrown out.

Divide

Whatever the approach, you will make many difficult choices. If you're like me you will be looking to wimp out regularly. I have found that making decisions by stages works best. I often divide junk and stuff into designated piles that accommodate my indecisiveness and resistance.

Pile #1: Junk. Where you collect the ugly, useless, energy-sucking objects that you know, without much doubt, to be junk.

Pile#2: Not Sure. Where, after honest consideration, you cannot decide yet whether to throw out, keep/fix, give away or sell.

Pile#3: Give Away or Sell. Where you identify what can be sold or, if that represents more time and effort than you're willing to invest, where you decide what can be given to family, friends, people in need or charitable organizations.

Pile#4: Keep For Relocation. Where you place items that you had to move in order to get at junk and will relocate at the end of the project.

Pile#5: Sentimental Things. Where your heart speaks louder than your head and refuses to let go of even the ugliest broken watch or rat-assed hat because of emotional attachment. At this point, contemplating these choices is a loser. Uses up time and energy that fails to move you ahead. Just put it in this pile for now.

Conquer

Before proceeding, throw the undeniable junk from Pile#1 all the way out. Do not review it. Do not allow it to reside in your garbage area awaiting the garbage truck. Either put it at the curb because today is garbage day or bring it to the dump yourself. Get it there today. This gives you a quick win, prevents backtracking (…that purple and yellow potholder might make a cute doily…) and clarifies choices yet to be made in the other piles. At this point a small reward or celebration is justified. Maybe a hamburger or tofu salad on the way home from the dump.

With the junk in Pile#1 gone forever, some of your choices in *Pile#2: Not Sure* may become clearer. Whether they do or not, revisit *Pile#2:Not Sure* from time to time, moving newly-identified junk to Pile#1. While you're at it, move potential give-away or sell items to Pile#3 and items for possible relocation to Pile#4. Eventually, Pile#2 will disappear.

Pile#3: Give Away or Sell, provides the opportunity to harmonize your needs with those of others. In deciding whether to give away or sell the items, remember the potlatch tradition of various indigenous cultures in North America. Potlatch and other giveaway ceremonies allow people to lighten the burden of their surplus possessions and practice generosity at the same time. Pile #3 can be the birth of your own personal and permanent potlatch.

Your perspective on the true worth of the items in *Pile#4: Keep For Relocation* will probably be improved as you separate junk from stuff in the other piles. By the end of the session it should be easier for you to decide which items in Pile#4 you will relocate and which items you will let go.

And so we come to perhaps the most vexing of all piles, #5: *Sentimental Things*, consisting of the beautiful and the ugly, the functional and the broken, the mended and the torn, the rigid and the droopy. Some of it drains and keeps us mired in the past. Some of it grounds and defines us, nourishing our souls. A broken clock conjures images of grandpa. A rag doll leaking foam restores the secure comforts of childhood. A plastic Mountie echoes a family trip to New Brunswick. A dirt-encrusted baseball still smells of Fenway Park.

Enough with the violins. There's only one way to handle this stalemate. Get rid of a third of it. Put the rest away in one place – bag, box or trunk. Visit every six months and get rid of another ten percent. Stop only when you begin to suffer the initial symptoms of vertigo. The removal of junk will make the nourishing items more apparent. Some of them may end up in circulation on mantles, side tables or shelves, in place of familiar but tired artifacts ready for rest or exile. Over time the increased space in your life will free your intuition to tell you, with increasing ease, what to keep and what to let go.

When you reach the point where you have processed and distributed the five piles, you have achieved a victory. Following years of taking you for granted, your possessions have been shaken out and subjected to your judgement. You have extended yourself physically, emotionally and spiritually. You deserve a break. And, before continuing, you may need to undergo withdrawal management.

6. A Word About Withdrawal Management

In the addictions field, withdrawal (detoxification) refers to the process whereby the body rids itself of the physical and psychological effects of alcohol and other drugs. Withdrawal from possessions can bring on some of the same symptoms of emotional imbalance as drug withdrawal: feelings of vulnerability, anxiety, ambivalence and craving for junk. Unpredictable in its effects, cleaning out can also bring on feelings of lightness and a fever to continue de-junking forever.

If you recognize any of these emotions, pause rather than panic. You are experiencing a kind of " fertile disorientation " brought on by the absence of familiar burdens and the presence of unfamiliar space. You are passing through a transition stage on the way to the planet Elbowroom, adjusting internally to the external changes you have created.

Remind yourself of your original reasons for simplifying your surroundings. Review your notes. Look at the bigger picture of your life and where you want to go. Remind yourself of all the work you have just completed in order to create more freedom for yourself. If necessary, call a friend and talk it out. And remember to celebrate.

Celebration is the best part of withdrawal management. Celebrating the end of a de-junking cycle can be as brief as a beer and a bratwurst in the back yard or as elaborate as a vacation in the mountains. Maybe a good movie or a barbecue with the people who helped you clean out. You can treat yourself to a commemorative talisman of some kind. A burnished stone, a ceramic Mayan God, a book about mountain climbing or a paperweight that looks like a gerbil can cement your attachment to what you have just accomplished and reinforce your intention to do it again.

Take a final tour of the battleground and reflect on the changes you have made. This is an appropriate time and setting for becoming conscious of your feelings of relief and accomplishment – perhaps some mixture of sadness and emptiness as well. Accept all the feelings. They belong in the transition that has been initiated around you and in you.

7. Ride Shotgun

One of the most romantic images I retain from childhood comes from the western movies that used to nourish and sustain me. Stagecoaches constantly made their way into and out of hostile territory where robbers and murderers lurked at the top of the cliff or behind the rock. Or atop the rock on the cliff. Sometimes they even pushed the rock off the cliff onto or in front of the coach. Anyway, the stagecoach had a driver and a guy with a rifle or shotgun whose job was to keep an eye out for bad guys. The lookout was said to ride shotgun.

When it comes to the accumulation of junk, we have to ride shotgun, to keep a lookout as we traverse a cultural environment that, at every turn, undermines our efforts to simplify. The marketplace offers us enormous quantity, browbeating us twenty-four hours a day to buy and consume, available space be damned. Come to think of it, they sell that too.

An eighty/twenty rule with wide application goes something like this: eighty percent of the value comes from twenty percent of the products. Or eighty percent of the productivity comes from twenty percent of the employees. Or eighty percent of the time we use twenty percent of what we own.

Here's one featuring an adjusted formula that recognizes the massive solicitation we face every day: far less than one percent of what we are being seduced to buy has any value for us whatsoever. And it will only get worse. While the storm is unstoppable, however, you can step outside of it as often as necessary. You can navigate its currents using five principles.

1. Quit permanently. To create room for your own renewal and to manage accelerating change, make letting go of junk a permanent feature of your life. You can create space in your schedule for regular de-junking festivals.

2. When something comes in, something goes out. You can reduce the need for de-junking by ensuring that accumulation of new stuff coincides with getting rid of junk. This is especially important in the case of clothes and information. Most of us wear less than ten percent of the clothes that we own. Reducing your clothing inventory and making a commitment to buy more selectively will increase your appreciation for what's left and steer you away from impulse buying.

Junk information can be looked at once and tossed out. The first surface that junk mail touches need not be a desk. It could be the bottom of a garbage can. You can use files, binders and shelves to store only information of value after the junk has been tossed. And you can unclog the public square where mail, bills, bank statements, magazines, calendars and reminders accumulate by setting aside a separate place to process only bills and banking.

3. Have a place for everything. You can put similar things in the same, predictable locations and keep them there. These allocated spaces can be limited so that when the space is filled you must decide which items to toss out rather than squeeze into another location. Dividers and small boxes in drawers can separate gadgets and other cute stuff. Old kettle cords can be pitched rather than piled in a basement box. No, the hydraulic breast enhancer cannot be used for boiling eggs.

4. Don't forget to say yes. In your efforts to clean out and say no to junk at the front end, don't forget to say yes to what feeds your soul. There is danger in becoming too good at riding shotgun, of overdeveloping your screening faculties. Do not omit juicy, messy and fun stuff. Know when enough is enough. Sometimes a pair of spray-painted work boots from sentimental times make good bookends.

5. Beware of time-management systems. Remember, time management is an agent of the machine. Get rid of any appointment book or time management system that leaves you with lists and categories of commitment that never arrive at empty. Avoid any system that steers you away from the most important commitments in your life

- time to sit by a stream, enjoy a good meal with your spouse, play with the kids without glancing at the watch, go to a movie or pluck your eyebrows.

When we take responsibility for removing clutter we reap benefits that go beyond physical space. We learn to breathe more freely and condition ourselves to enjoying and defending that freedom. As we integrate simplifying into our lives, we sensitize ourselves to the difference between junk and stuff at the front end and reduce the need to fight it at the back end.

CHAPTER FOUR

GIVE YOURSELF THE TIME AND SPACE TO PROCESS YOUR LIFE

"There never was a great character who did not sometimes smash the routine regulations, and make new ones for himself."

Andrew Carnegie

1. Steer Your Boat and Let the Sea Take Care of Itself

Triton is the sea-god of Greek mythology who controls the sea by blowing his conch-shell horn once in a while. We all sail our little boats on Triton's sea but overload ourselves when we try to control currents, winds and storm fronts that are beyond our powers. By acting as if we play the magic conch-shell, we squander energy and creativity that could be applied to moving in interesting and fulfilling directions.

It's a paradox. Life flows unconditionally and invites us to play. But participating in ways that assume we can control all of the flow undermines our ability to participate fully. It's the difference between pushing with ego and being guided by spirit.

When we push with ego, we are conscious of the world around us but live under the illusion that what we see is all there is. At the same time, we fear the unknown and what could happen. We pursue security by trying unsuccessfully to control too much. This struggle keeps us busy but obscures our sense of direction. We work against perceived time constraints and a sense of undefined urgency, jumping from task to task without asking why.

Being guided by spirit, on the other hand, animates us. We accept that we need not anticipate and define everything. We recognize that each of us plays our part in the developing big picture and that an essential aspect of the voyage is the ongoing discovery of what that part is. We work with time's flow and learn to trust our ability to self-organize as we go. We recognize our power to steer our boats according to life's currents.

Seeing beyond anxieties and accepting our lives as part of a larger process allows us to more consistently ground ourselves and gain access to creativity as a directional force. This involves trusting our intuitive ability to see what is significant and to separate our fears and less important outside demands from items that attract our passion and genuine interest. The mind that's obsessed with controlling the uncontrollable dries up. It cannot reach for its dreams because it cannot dream.

I recently viewed, yet again, one of my favourite episodes from the 90's television series *Northern Exposure*. Ed Chicliak is a young man in the town of Cicely, Alaska, who wants to become a movie director. But during most of the episode he makes excuses for not starting the movie script that can move him toward his dream.

Movie director Peter Bogdanovich, with whom Ed has an e-mail correspondence, flies to Alaska to confer with his young friend. During a walk in the woods, Peter suggests that Ed make a movie to reduce his stress, insomnia and stomach problems. Shifting his eyes, Ed replies that he's too busy studying to be a shaman.

The show's climactic scene involves a conversation between Ed and an elder named Leonard as they view Orson Welles' classic movie *Citizen Kane*. Ed comments that it is actually a movie within a movie. Whereas Welles' character in the movie starts a newspaper just for fun and without any expertise, the real-life Welles made *Citizen Kane* without knowing where he was going. He just did it to fulfill his vision. Admiring Welles' fearlessness, Ed says, "He didn't know what he was doing yet he did something that was perfect. Makes you think about what's possible."

But he despairs: "Before long the movie will be over and I still won't know what to do with my life. I'm really confused, Leonard." Leonard finally lances the boil: "Maybe this is it. The path to our destination is not always a straight one, Ed. We go down the wrong road, we get lost, we turn back. Maybe it doesn't matter what road we embark on. Maybe what matters is that we embark."

In the show's final scene, the camera lens sweeps upward and we see Ed's expanding smile as his dancing fingertips and the clacking typewriter dispel the clouds of confusion.

Makes you think about what's possible.

2. Make Time Serve You

On his credenza
There is a tangle of bronze birds
Too heavy to fly.

On one corner of his desk
A mahogany sailing boat
He never sails.

> *On another corner of his desk*
> *A chrome rimmed portrait of a family*
> *He has never known.*

> *And sitting in his chair*
> *A tangle of brass*
> *Too heavy to fly.*

Many of us can identify with the thick individual sitting as the "tangle of brass" in the chair of John Butler's poem, *Office Décor*. [1] We feel numb in proportion to the frequency with which we put aside our needs in order to give away chunks of time to someone else's urgency. The more time and energy we devote rushing to meet these demands the less likely we are to reflect on why we do it and how it fits our vision of where we want to go.

When we see time as limited we are more likely to serve it as our master on the assumption that we have no alternative. Deep down we know we have alternatives but may hesitate to explore them, stripping ourselves of one of our most essential and precious attributes, the ability to choose. Time as master means:

Chasing somebody else's priorities,
Never-ending deadlines and shortages of time,
Permanent anxiety about the future,
Defensiveness, cover your ass, try not to screw up,

Short-term responses rather than long-term solutions.

Making time serve us requires that we step back and carve it up in ways that liberate our energy, creativity and ability to take full advantage of unexpected opportunities. When we make time a servant we see it as abundant, we let our inner voice guide us toward what counts and we give the important things the time they need. We spend more time being passionately involved in the present moment and feel a greater sense of relaxation, openness and positive expectation.

Any of us could list dozens of barriers that keep us from mastering time. From the outside, we are subjected to unexpected calls, people who drop in, crises created by chaotic colleagues, social gatherings, family duties, slave-driver bosses, broken-down cars, lawnmowers that refuse to mow and dishwashers that refuse to wash dishes. From the inside, we encounter our own limitations. We can try to do too much, get lost in detail because of perfectionism and have difficulty saying no. We can be disorganized, lack direction and leave tasks unfinished. We can feel trapped by our own make-up.

Choosing to exercise the power to define our own time may require some reflection because, at times, being busy may be less an indication of irresistible outside demands than a tool for avoiding things that we find unpleasant. Busy-ness may allow someone who wants to be liked to avoid additional work responsibilities without having to refuse. It can deflect the short-term discomfort of having to express intimacy and deal with relationship issues. It can save someone who feels self-worth only through struggle from having to experience the guilt of stillness and exposure to the scary notion that more is accomplished through flow than through forcing.

Taking over the driver's seat can be a major step. It requires a genuine commitment beyond good intentions. The following questions may help you to clarify your relationship to busy-ness.

1. Do you feel uncomfortable when you are not busy? Do your feelings of self-worth come primarily from yourself or others?

2. Does being busy help you to avoid doing things you do not want to do? Do you have difficulty saying no? Do you wish you could spend more time with family or friends?

3. Do you wish that you could have more control over how you spend your time? Do you think it possible? Are you doing anything now to achieve more control of your time or are you looking to do it at some point in the future?

We can't count on the magic transformation in ourselves or the breakthrough in time-management technology that will set us free. And forget about the world's return to a rational pace. Ain't gonna happen. Only we as individuals can slow time down and make it serve us. We can do it by accepting responsibility for designing how we metabolize time in the same way that we determine what food we eat or what clothes we wear. We can start by trusting ourselves and gradually letting go of whatever interferes with who we want to be and what we want to do.

3. Clean Out Your Cave

In many cultures, the bat is a symbol for the rebirth that follows the death of obsolete patterns. Shamans in these cultures must undergo the ritualistic death of old identities in order to prepare themselves for the assumption of new identities. Most of us may choose not to spend a night quaking in an open grave or hanging upside down in a cave but our rites of passage do require that we let go of obstacles to our development. As the death of old patterns creates room for the new, dismantling obsolete commitments and structures provides space for reaching deeper levels of creativity. Here are nine ways to clean out your cave:

1. De-schedule. Gradually reduce the items on your schedule that fail to stimulate your passionate involvement. Reduce the time you invest in causes or committees where a select few control the energy, resources and decision-making. If you believe that you cannot change this arrangement, look for alternatives that make better use of your gifts. Get used to scheduling empty space into your day. There will always be more that you could plan and do. You can multiply your ability to get more done just by getting rid of the useless baggage.

2. Learn to say no. An urgent demand is not necessarily an important demand. Setting limits on what you can accomplish each day can allow you to more consistently refuse the urgent but unimportant. This sets the stage for paying quality attention to what matters most. People often respond yes when they mean no because they fear offending someone or undermining their own social or work status. Saying no is a choice. Say it quickly and pleasantly. Explain but do not defend yourself. Occasionally, you can say no for now, pending developments or your need to reflect on the request. Often the situation will go away. You can practice ways of saying no by yourself until you get them right.

3. Let somebody else do it better. One of the reasons many of us suffer from overload stems from the difficulty we have letting go of tasks that we feel we can do better. If you too suffer from this illusion, review the responsibilities and tasks that you now have. Use three questions to help you determine which of them you will keep: Where do my best talents lie? What do I most want to learn? What feeds my passion and lets me have fun?

Identifying our best bits puts us in a better position to be honest with ourselves concerning what others can do better. Be clear and positive rather than hesitant in negotiating and handing over the responsibilities and tasks. The importance of this process goes beyond you. It increases the chances that the group, family, company or community will be served by a more productive distribution of labour based on its members' strengths.

4. Give procrastination a chance to be your friend. We know we are putting off unpleasant tasks when we feel exhausted just thinking about them, have difficulty taking the first or final steps and avoid them by doing other things. Some of the guilt we feel arises from the assumption that these tasks are worth doing.

But sometimes we resist for good reason. Procrastination can be a protection against doing too much and a signal that it's time to examine the work list to see if it fits with the purpose and direction that is most important for us. When you procrastinate, examine the demands being made on you by answering these questions: Are they worth doing in the first place? Are they somebody else's responsibility? Can trade-offs be made?

Take your cue from the answers to these questions and your inner voice. Throw or negotiate away as many as you can of the tasks that fail to pass the test. You will probably not clear the slate entirely but a few key drop-offs from time to time represent important victories and reinforce new conditioning that can gradually lead to more creative choices in the first place.

5. Invest less time in meetings. Ask yourself if the meeting is really necessary. Can you get it done with a conference call? Do you use meetings as security blankets? Learn to make decisions without having a meeting. Know when to make a group decision and when to make an individual decision. If you have to have a meeting, be prepared, set a time limit, have an agenda and invite only those people whose attendance is necessary. Have somebody take concise minutes. Invest the time you save on meetings in taking care of yourself and the people you love.

6. Reject constipation by communication. Telephone, fax and e-mail make communicating with the world easier than making toast. Trouble is, it goes both ways. Like incoming information materials, much communication is unnecessary. Separate the nuggets from the rocks by screening incoming messages and controlling any insecurities that insist you must respond to all of them. You can screen messages according to three lists: must, could and might. Then you can throw out the might list and two-thirds of the could list. Make the remaining calls and be open to reducing the lists further as you clarify your definitions of essential and important.

By the way, try to avoid sending people unnecessary information, such as the witty three-page discourse on the significance of the fall solstice in your planning cycle. Not that there's anything wrong with that. Pick your correspondents carefully and treat them well. That's what friends are for.

7. Do nothing of importance on Mondays. Mondays come after Saturdays and Sundays. On those days most of us fly free of schedules and the insistent drumbeat of the workplace. Some of us fly hard and some of us glide. But on Monday morning we lurch back into our cages. The transition can be brutal. More people have heart attacks or strokes on Mondays than on any other day. Monday is the most popular day for having work-related accidents or committing suicide. Not a good day for mental activity and intense interaction. Try to treat it as a transition day. Hang out with people who make you laugh. There will be time enough for seriousness on Tuesday.

8. Muck out regularly. The need to clean out and tie up loose ends is always with us. Try to set aside at least half a day each week to muck out information, communications and paperwork. Take an inventory of your accumulated material and put it where it belongs. Much of it, including the items on the floor, will no longer be required and can be thrown out or given away.

9. Get used to throwing junk out at the front end. Information storage systems exist for any orientation. They enable us to take inventory, assess the results and determine unlimited ways of organizing our information. As previously indicated, they enable us to place frequently-used items within easy reach. They help us to separate materials for different projects. They supply endless variations of trays designed to prevent nasty spillage. But they tend not to address the step that enables it all to work – the first step: throwing out as much of the information as possible when it comes in. Like a good, blue-chip investment, this simple habit may take time to cultivate but can bring compound returns in the form of the space necessary to enable efficiency systems to work the way they should.

If you have an extreme need to clean out your cave, you may have been putting off self-care as well. During or after cave-cleaning, walk away and do something just for the fun of it. No guilt. Go for a walk, take a long lunch, go to a movie, buy the marmoset you've been eyeballing. Go home early and take a nap. Renewal is not a reward, it's a right and a necessity. A clean cave serves the shaman in all of us.

4. While You're At It, Get Rid of the Vampires in Your Life

Where bats symbolize the death of the obsolete and the birth of the new, the vampires in our lives merely symbolize death. Vampire people elevate their desires far above those of others and address others' needs primarily to draw attention and energy to themselves. They come in many forms, including the clowns, the bullies, the risk-takers, the helpless and the workaholics. They use a range of tactics, from intimidation, deception and seduction to charisma, perpetual busy-ness and demands for perfection.

While they may initially stimulate us, the net effect of their melodramas is to deplete us. Here is a more detailed look at a few types and some ways to protect your energies:

Crisis Junkies. We all face challenges with heavy workloads and deadlines. So we can sympathize with someone who approaches us for help in coping with those demands. But we can also draw a line between helping a colleague and being pulled into his or her quicksand.

Some people are addicted to crisis and stress. They constantly struggle to complete the urgent work thrust upon them even as they agree to take on more urgent work thrust upon them. Instead of reflecting, they react. Instead of thinking ahead, they race ahead. To protect your time, inoculate yourself against crisis junkies by avoiding the urge to rescue them. The opportunity to experience the consequences of their indiscriminate racing may even prompt them to make their own changes.

Pa Kettles. Pa Kettle was a character in a series of movies that presented the zany adventures of the Kettle family. You can still rent the movies or watch them on television at 3:05 in the morning. Though loveable, Pa's main occupation was avoiding work by hiding or getting somebody else to do it. Take Pa Kettles off your dance card.

Pa Kettles exist on the same continuum as crisis junkies. Each responds to others' priorities but, whereas crisis junkies race blindly into perpetuity, Pa Kettles fill their time concentrating on time-wasting activities having little importance. Whereas crisis junkies can have a hyper sense of responsibility, Pa Kettles avoid it as much as possible and, in loveable ways, unload it on you. Crisis junkies wear you down with action and panic. Pa Kettles smother you with cushions. Avoid being so needy for crackerbarrel comfort that you carry Pa on your shoulders.

Performers seek the spotlight because they identify themselves primarily through the eyes of others. Appearances are very important to them, the undivided attention of others their lifeline. They have difficulty tolerating other people being the centre of attention and will seek to deflect that attention to themselves, either subtly or by waiting for the opportunity to discount the views of whoever happens to occupy the spotlight. They often put themselves in a controlling position by using the gentle arts of attention, flattery and seduction to maneuver someone into a leaning position, similar to a dog getting a rub behind the ears.

In the sexual arena this seduction can become complicated when the leaning party tries to take un-negotiated liberties and is rebuffed with shocked surprise by the seducing party. In Transactional Analysis circles this game is known as Now I've Got You, You Sonofabitch. Detach from the game so that you can see it clearly and decide if there's anything constructive to be accomplished while it's happening. Either leave or, in a positive but firm way, change the subject. Do not participate in the game.

Perfectionists carry a lot of anger related to the difference between how perfect life could be and how imperfect and chaotic it is. They live in a permanent state of tension because of the mistakes that are always being made despite their best efforts to catch and correct them. Imperfection makes them feel vulnerable and out of control, and they find it difficult to allow others the space to make mistakes or do things in unapproved ways.

When sober they do not have much fun because of their difficulty in letting go of the worry that accompanies the pursuit of the best way to do everything. They are constantly demanding and critical of themselves and others, and can be difficult bosses because their relationships with subordinates often replay the conflicts they have within themselves. Genuine two-way communication suffers.

When communicating with perfectionists, establish a protective buffer by projecting confidence. Be specific in sharing your value system, point of view and boundaries. After you've gained their respect, make them laugh once in a while. They'll appreciate the breather.

Some folks consume less of our life force than others. You can maintain communication with bitchy relatives and difficult neighbours on an occasional rather than intimate basis. Childhood friends who want to rewind school days can be nice for an hour rather than a day. Some co-workers are fun over Christmas eggnog while others make enjoyable companions for regular evenings out. Telling some folks that you want to spend less or no time with them is cold unless you are provoked. But keeping conversations brief, having a coffee instead of dinner and telling them honestly that you have other commitments are respectful ways to modify your commitments.

Most of these descriptions are, of course, pure stereotypes. Most vampire people combine these and other qualities, including positive ones. On occasion, most of us play the role of vampires. But we all live with the reality that some people carry more importance in our lives than others and we must decide who they are. Making these choices is important because time taken from vampires means time spent on personal priorities and with people we like, respect and love.

5. Keep It In Perspective by Reflecting on Bugs and Sam From Time to Time

The previous piece may have seemed harsh. After all, dealing with difficult people provides opportunities to sharpen our identities, priorities and communication skills. Let's look at the issue in a more gentle way, using one of our culture's foremost models of self-determination, perseverance and joyful living – Bugs Bunny.

If he's not digging a hole in Kentucky that comes out on a golf course in Scotland, Bugs can be seen rowing to Europe or performing as a matador for the Tasmanian Devil. Steal an inch from him and he will get that back with ten miles' interest. Not that he wants to hurt anybody. He just has a vision that includes living joyfully in the moment, whether it's on a golf course, in a hammock or in the depths of Sherwood Forest.

Despite his prominence though, Bugs' star would not shine as brightly without the uncooperative shenanigans of the most underrated character in the history of animation, Yosemite Sam. More complex than most cartoon villains, Sam represents our own cantankerous sides and the adversarial forces that we all have to face in trying to live our lives to the full. He's sort of a pink and red Darth Vader.

In the face of Yosemite Sam's imposing presence, Bugs goes about his business of smelling life's roses, whether that means digging tunnels, eating carrots or simply enjoying the outdoors during hunting season. Sam tries to interfere with these harmless activities and beyond that, with Bugs' well being. With his fearful temper and permanently-outraged appearance, he constitutes a major threat to the buck-toothed one. Or does he?

Bugs' most important strengths include self-confidence and deep intelligence. He avoids overestimating Sam's negative capabilities and, in fact, handles him rather easily, turning the tables on him time and again. But harming Yosemite Sam is not the main point. The big payoff for Bugs is the continued enjoyment of what life provides without obstructions. Spending all his time trying to outdo Sam would be self-defeating. Sam does, however, keep Bugs from taking life's beauty for granted.

In the form of people, events and our inner demons we all face Yosemite Sams. They are a constant presence and they help us to decide on how we will balance dealing with obstructions and living our lives to the full.

Elmer Fudd doesn't help us to do that. After all, who can be motivated by a guy who wears that ridiculous hat?

6. Live on Purpose

One of the most repeated entries on lists of influential and inspiring books of the twentieth century is *Man's Search For Meaning* by Viktor Frankl. An Austrian psychiatrist, Frankl was imprisoned for three years in Auschwitz and other German prison camps, losing his possessions and almost all of his family. Subjected to endless brutality and hunger, he never knew if and when his life would be taken from him. Yet, from incomprehensible horror, he wrote a book about optimism and freedom. We find its essence in Frankl's belief that between what happens to us and our response is a space where we choose what that response will be. Our growth and our freedom flourishes from the choices we make in that space. [2]

I think Frankl is saying that, regardless of circumstances, we always have more choices than we know. We have the ability to decide how outside influences will affect us and how we will bring meaning to our activities. Living on purpose means choosing our paths consciously and participating fully in the subsequent activities that are most important to us - that support who we want to be, that enhance our maturity and that help others. Living on purpose requires that we tap the values and inner voice that connect us to a deeper level of intelligence - our real power base. Sometimes this requires waiting and sometimes it requires action.

1. Dig yourself up. To introduce yourself to your deepest thoughts, start a notebook or journal where you regularly write for stretches lasting at least fifteen minutes. Keep the pen, pencil or keys moving without planning ahead. Do not erase mistakes. Do not worry about spelling or grammar. Just get it down. If you keep your critical judge out of the exercise, the writing can come from a deep place, often hidden by daily distractions. Do this at least a couple of times a week when you are unrushed. Morning is a good time. Get used to loosening up your subconscious in this way and occasionally re-visit your writings. What themes concern you most? What do they have in common?

2. *Know when to wait on decisions.* Our work ethic says that decisions need to be made quickly and that hesitation signifies weakness. Sometimes it does. Much of the time, though, decisions can wait. Pause and make choices consciously, in accordance with your values and sense of what is right. Let the big picture emerge. Relaxing away from issues, even for a few minutes, gives our right-brain intuitive faculties a chance to function. Ideas and solutions get a chance to surface on their own because patience exposes us to more creative capacity. Take as many timeouts as you need or can get away with.

3. *Recognize decisions that carry more risk.* Spend more time thinking about decisions that are uncertain or carry a greater risk of producing regret. This will differ among individuals. For most folks, buying a car brings more concern than buying a shirt. In my case, picking the shirt has always presented a bigger challenge.

4. *Know when to toss a coin.* Some decisions are not worth a lot of time. If you find yourself grinding your molars over a choice between brands of toothpaste for sensitive teeth, toss a coin and learn from the subsequent experience. There's something to be said for moving on.

Living on purpose requires contemplation and action, two essential parts of the same thing. Contemplation works best when intuition and logic can cooperate without the interference of urgency or negative beliefs. Mindful action requires that, having made the decision to proceed, we commit ourselves without hesitation, accepting both the positive and negative consequences and learning from the experience as a way of informing future choices.

7. Move From the Bottom of the List to the Centre of the Circle

I spent too many years discovering, again and again, the solutions to my racing and chasing. It all began with three columns on a piece of paper. In the left column I listed the essential tasks to be completed that day. Tasks that must be completed. Had to be completed. Could not be not completed. That day.

The middle column listed important but non-essential tasks. Any of the tasks left uncompleted today could be completed tomorrow, possibly under the left column or, if things got worse, under the third column, the one on the right containing optional tasks that could be done today or not, depending on time left from the essential and more important tasks in the middle and left columns. Each column listed tasks in descending order of priority, the most essential, important or doable at the top.

It turned out that, on a good day, I completed between five and fifteen percent of the items in the first column. That is, unless I decided to relieve the pressure by beavering in one of the other columns for a while. Either way, I experienced a permanent state of stress trying to keep up, and a discouraging sense that nothing was ever being accomplished.

I eventually went to a two-column system – essential and important. Same stress and frustration but no optional playpen. I found myself viewing the worlds of work and home through lenses coloured important, urgent, essential and you'll-die-if-you-don't. I finally crushed this arrangement into one long column, screening the entries but still having no hope of completion. Same permanent state of dread focusing on the undone with no time to enjoy completions.

I read time-management books and participated in seminars, repeatedly finding solutions to my cramming obsessions. I catalogued reference materials with bookmarks, on loose pieces of paper and post-it notes, placing them on shelves, in carefully labeled piles on the floor and in file folders tucked into groaning cabinets. My time-management arsenal took its place beside, on top of and under other mountains of information. The miracles of fax machine and computer only raised the water level while widening the floodgates.

In despair, I would occasionally revert to my original system for coping with time and information crises. Forget the lists, ignore selected memos, avoid as many useless meetings as possible and allow documents to accumulate until the piles became high enough to qualify for dumping into a wastebasket or garbage can. Despite creating some professional relationship problems, this system proved superior to the multi-column approach. It freed up time, reduced energy drain and occasionally cleaned up the desk. For about an hour. Inventing and reinventing ways to catch the balls being tossed at me missed the point. Self-organizing became the largest part of the problem.

Lists can be self-organization traps that steer us away from, rather than toward, what is most important. Unless we pause and control our attention long enough to focus on what really counts, lists can reinforce the hierarchical thinking that places our personal priorities in the basement. When we think hierarchically we see tasks in descending order of importance, with the most important tasks at the top. Hierarchical thinking always sees the straight line as the shortest distance between two points, maintains that there is a beginning and an end to everything and holds that tasks must be accomplished in sequence, where task one precedes task two which precedes task three and so on.

We fall into a trap when we set up lists that tell us we can take care of our own needs only after we have met outside demands. This straight-line orientation says that we move toward our priorities as we descend the list, crossing off the important tasks as we complete them. Two problems crop up over time. First, the top section of the list becomes increasingly dominated by urgent tasks whose importance we may exaggerate. Second, we never seem to get to our items because the list never seems to arrive at the bottom. Our destination keeps moving away as we try to reach it. The following agenda illustrates the point.

1. *Catch up on calls, correspondence*
2. *Two-hour meeting*
3. *Working lunch*
4. *Attend seminar*
5. *Prepare presentation*
6. *Exercise*
7. *Early dinner*
8. *Mow lawn*
9. *Rest and read*
10. *Movie with friends*

Our items at the end of the list end up being sugar-cube rewards for serving the previous catalogue of requirements. As a result, many of our personal aspirations reside permanently in the future and often not even there, when we use the exercise, dinner, lawn-mowing and movie/downtime to catch up on previous items that have not been completed.

Relational thinking can cut through the bureaucracy of hierarchical thinking and connect us more directly to what feeds our souls. In *Surfing The Himalayas*, [3] Frederick Lenz describes relational thinking as the perception of things from a point of stillness in the mind, which eliminates extraneous noise and taps into all layers of consciousness, allowing us to more easily identify new connections and what matters most. According to Lenz, the most successful people are those who think relationally rather than hierarchically.

When we see relationally, we recognize everything as connected to everything else and view ourselves as the prime initiators and decision-makers in our lives. We see life expanding as a spiral, in never-ending cycles. And we realize that sometimes the shortest distance between two points is a circle with us in the centre, choosing from among alternatives without having to take intermediate steps if we do not see the need.

From our vantage point at the centre, we see all of our options at the same time. We look at them directly, examining our relationship with the respective items based on where we are and what we need now. We are better able to balance the pressures from outside with our immediate needs because our needs have equal status within the circle.

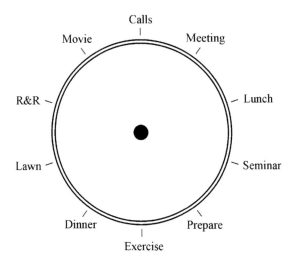

In seeing all items at once in relation to us and in their relation to each other, we can determine more clearly how the tasks connect to our needs and organize our lists or schedules accordingly. For example, we may be able to shorten the two-hour meeting, cancel the working lunch and postpone preparation for the presentation, which is still three days away. Then we can spend the afternoon gossiping with the grocer, wandering bookstores, walking in the woods, reading or doing nothing. After dinner we can go to the movie in a relaxed frame of mind, having worked hard in the morning and idled all afternoon.

The point here is not to avoid responsibilities. It is to place ourselves and our relationships in the driver's seat - to make our personal agenda at least as important as the world's by introducing our imagination to decision-making and looking at our options through beginner's eyes rather than social conditioning.

If you have not already done so, make a habit of relational thinking. Take five minutes and a sheet of paper. Draw a big circle and divide it into four quadrants. Enter one of the following headings in each quadrant: Socializing/Family, Downtime/Solitude, Maintenance/ Repairs and Work/Volunteer. Along the surface of each quadrant, enter three to five tasks or activities that you feel you must do or want very much to do over the next week.

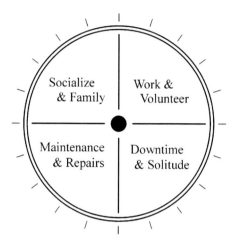

Now throw out at any of these items that you realize, upon reflection, have less importance or less urgency. Choose at least two items from each quadrant, giving the musts and the wants equal status. Either do them now or schedule them over the next week.

Putting yourself at the centre of the circle does not replace the need to move in straight lines or complete urgent and important tasks. But it can enable you, in a few minutes of reflection, to mobilize your intuition and balance your thinking. Whether you prefer to work on one task at a time or bounce among several, using relational thinking can help you to separate your true choices and responsibilities from those time-consumers and overrated demands that spring from pressure and inaccurate assumptions about what is important.

8. Get Rhythm

Everything in life is always changing - from the cells in our bodies, to the flowers in the fields and the galaxies in space. The life of a star, the progression of a year and our movement through a day always advance through four eternally-interacting cycles of energy: beginnings, growth, retreat and dormancy. The Sioux Holy Man Black Elk said,

"Even the seasons form a great circle in their changing, and always come back again to where they were. The life of a man is a circle from childhood to childhood and so it is in everything where power moves." [4]

We can make the most of our energy cycles and the seasons of our lives by living in harmony with these continuously fluctuating rhythms:

Beginnings, like spring, may follow a period of retreat, rest, play and preparation – or a dark night of the soul during which we have wrestled with self-doubt and confusion. When we emerge, we feel physically stronger, possess sharper mental clarity and express ourselves more freely. We sprout new interests and confidence, prepared to bring a new sense of optimism to our relationship with the world.

Growth, like summer, means action and fast-paced progress toward our dreams and making a positive difference. Confident in our bodies, we feel greater sensuality, trust and openness. We learn new things, heal emotional wounds and more easily express love and compassion. We energize others with our optimistic energy. Feeling that the universe is with us, we connect to the sacred pulse within and around us. We are on a roll.

Retreat, like autumn, follows the period of accelerated growth and allows us time for solitude and contemplation during which we reflect on what we have accomplished, review the lessons we have learned and clarify our purpose. We become more conscious of our body's need for rest and the importance of emotional relief. We have the opportunity to reach a higher level of spiritual maturity by seeing our beliefs, aspirations, accomplishments and frustrations in a less self-centred way, as part of a larger process.

Dormancy in nature comes during winter but, like the other stages, is available to us every day. A period of lying fallow, pause for its own sake, it renews us through cleansing, rest and fun. It gives us the perspective to appreciate our gifts and accept life on its terms. During this cycle we let go of obsolete possessions, attitudes and relationships. Refreshed and stabilized, we emerge with new commitment to self-care and sharing.

The worldviews of societies throughout the world contain variations of these cycles. For example, they form the basis for the Native American Medicine Wheel. They are also reflected in the yin-yang polarities of Chinese civilization, where ch'i is seen as the creative force underlying all life, unfolding through continuous movement between the complementary polarities of yin and yang. Receptive yin represents retreat and dormancy in all its manifestations, and active yang represents beginnings and rapid growth. We are all subject to these rhythms but possess our individual differences.

Night people, for example, may derive the best level of daily energy by going to sleep at midnight or one a.m. and getting up between seven and eight a.m. These owls may not be fully awake until mid-morning. For morning people, on the other hand, the best scenario may be closer to seven hours shut-eye between ten p.m. and five a.m. These larks are more likely to be fully awake by early morning. For the lark, a nine a.m. conference may be ideal. For the owl, it is more likely to be an ordeal unlike, say, an evening meeting.

Whether we fit the description of night owls, morning larks, spontaneous rabbits or deliberate turtles, we fluctuate among extremes every day. We move through physical stamina, strength and dexterity to low energy, sleepiness and clumsiness. We bounce from alertness, good judgement and mental retention to lack of focus, mental dullness and back again. At some points, life seems a journey in serenity and optimism. A little farther down the road, our positive expectations evaporate in the heat of a hostile world.

The shift in these cycles can happen within a few minutes or a couple of hours. By increasing our awareness of the fluctuations we can improve our ability to flow with the currents rather than struggle against them. When we feel less physical stamina, we can rest or take light exercise. Reduced alertness and judgement may signal the opportunity for mindless or meditative activity. Hostile cycles may tell us that we should slow down, contemplate and plan our next moves carefully. On the other hand, we can accomplish more demanding challenges by taking advantage of our up cycles.

Before the industrial revolution, societies and individuals were more influenced by a view of life tied to nature's cycles. The sun, moon, tides and seasons dictated the ebb and flow of life – a time to plant, a time to reap, a time to celebrate and a time to lie fallow. The cycles of people's lives and nature's rhythms were connected. But the elevation of production, wealth-creation and efficiency created a distance between humanity and nature's rhythms. People began to obey clocks more and nature less. Our natural rhythms became secondary considerations.

Daily efforts to stay afloat in today's torrent of speed, information and violence can promote the feeling that fragmentation and exhaustion are natural. We don't have to accept this sacred cow. We possess the power to gradually detach ourselves from the conditioning that keeps us racing. Here are seven ways to surf daily pressures rather than drown in them:

1. Avoid trying to do everything every day. Don't do the same things every day. Don't do things in the same sequence every day. Whether you are lark or owl, rabbit or turtle, take the time to gradually align your daily responsibilities with your natural cycles.

2. Always expect the unexpected. Leave empty spaces in your schedule for the unexpected, which usually appears as an opportunity, a crisis or a combination of the two. Sometimes it comes out of the blue and sometimes it arises out of your own efforts. The unexpected always reminds us that our ability to control the river of life is severely limited and that the unforeseen is the most powerful cycle of all.

3. Renew yourself every day by getting out of your head and into your heart and body. Renewal lets us move from thinking and doing to feeling and being. The active form involves physical exertion, play and socializing. The passive form includes idleness, aimlessness and solitude. Balance self-worth stemming from work with unconditional love for yourself. Make taking care of yourself a daily agenda item until it becomes automatic.

4. Take time to reflect. Even if they only last a few minutes, allow yourself the unhurried periods that you need to review your progress and consolidate your thoughts. Open yourself to spontaneous inspiration, intuitive insights and meaningful coincidence. As often as you can, schedule time for nothing but reflection. During these breaks, refuse to be rushed by artificial deadlines.

5. Give beginnings and transitions the time they need. Beginnings require nurturing and patience before they flower. Whether this involves learning a new skill, developing a new relationship or adopting unfamiliar behaviours, give yourself the opportunity to gradually let go of old patterns and establish solid foundations for new growth. They don't usually happen overnight.

6. Give yourself the time to prepare. When deadlines, information overload and too many priorities demand immediate attention, we often reduce or sacrifice the preparation cycle. As a result, we can rush to solutions that create new generations of problems. Preparation cycles cultivate creativity and increase the likelihood of mindful action and keeper solutions. Give yourself more preparation time by throwing out activities that are weeds in your garden.

7. Spend about twenty percent of your time restoring order. Allow yourself timeout cycles where you let go of obsolete possessions, useless information and vampire people. Re-organize what's left in new ways that complement where you want to go. Close any loose ends that get between you and relaxation by finishing projects, putting away tools and ending any memberships and subscriptions that no longer suit you. While you're at it, examine yourself for negative and pessimistic attitudes that can creep in from time to time, and drop them like rotten fish. Restoring order daily, weekly and at other regular intervals is essential to our clarity, flexibility and the ongoing ability to transform our lives.

When we operate according to our natural rhythms we bring ourselves more fully into the present. We conduct our lives with less distraction and more awareness of what we need. And we move closer to being our true selves because we swim with rather than against ourselves.

9. Be an Outsider

Being cool used to be cooler. It has deteriorated badly since Miles Davis, Gerry Mulligan, Gil Evans and others gave it voice through the evolution of a new jazz form in the late 1940's. Its deterioration tells us about ourselves and the world.

Cool referred to a way of living with integrity, spontaneity and passion. It implied a person who was self-aware, knowledgeable, graceful and humble, someone searching for his or her essential self wherever it might lead, regardless of mainstream society's standards. Cool meant keeping your eyes open and making the most of what you had in every situation, even if you felt lost and uncertain.

Cool valued flow and creation over fighting and forcing. It embraced openness to the voices in the wind and in your heart, and sharing what you knew and had with others walking their particular paths. At the beginning, it had nothing to do with image. It had nothing to do with purchase. It could not be given to you. You had to live it.

Cool's meaning has flipped. Less a reflection of individual integrity these days, it has deteriorated into an instrument of commerce that urges us to fit in by keeping up with cutting-edge fashion. It has become an attitude for covering up uncertainty and lack of self-knowledge by striking an image of detachment and self-sufficiency. And it's easy because it's for sale.

Much of our lives revolves around the current rendition of cool. Corporations sell the myth of liberation through purchase and consumption of products that let us feel as if we surf on the leading wave of the next big thing. Whether it's computers, t-shirts, automobiles, shaving technology, khaki pants advertised by Jack Kerouac or myriad products promising the rub-off effect from wealthy jock-heroes, we are being conditioned to equate individual expression with loyalty to brand names.

On the way into a shopping mall one day I met a young man, maybe 14 years old, who was wearing a beautiful t-shirt with the image of Che Guevera on the front in explosive yellows, oranges and reds. In passing I told him I liked the t-shirt. After walking about eight steps I turned and asked him if he knew who was depicted on the front. He didn't know, so I told him it was Che Guevera and asked him if he'd ever heard of him. After a short hesitation, the youngster replied, "Didn't he fight the machine?"

I said yes and related a brief story of Che the Cuban schoolteacher who became a warrior to fight for what he believed in, eventually dying for it in the mountains of Bolivia. The young man looked interested but I couldn't be sure. As I walked away, I wondered whether Che's image would sharpen his awareness or merely continue to decorate his body with colourful, anti-machine corporate cool. After all, why go to the discomfort of non-conformity and rebellion when you can buy it and wear it?

So how can cool be flipped back to its original meaning?

Realize that if you strive to be cool you won't be. If you project yourself as cool, you're not. Accept that you are your own message, not a billboard for somebody else's. Being an authentic person is both a painful and joyful trip. Discover your gifts by using them. Get to know who you are and what you believe in by moving toward it every day. Do not wear clothing with corporate names or logos as a substitute for self-discovery.

Accept your inherent weirdness, don't import it. Regardless of your age, be yourself in all your glorious uniqueness. Let yourself be an outsider regularly. Forget about keeping up - make the mainstream fit you. It is peripheral people who change the world most profoundly. Einstein and Churchill were strong individuals and preoccupied students whose teachers worried about their mental capacities. Einstein was so consumed by his own thoughts that he occasionally walked out of the house without his pants.

Outsiders do not wait for something to become cool in order to enjoy it. And they do not hide behind hip disdain when they do enjoy it. Don't be afraid to be a cliché. Appreciate loved ones who put up with your crap every day. Don't be self-conscious because mom still has the answers that mean so much to you. Let the lump rise in your throat when the cute puppy is rescued from the burning building or when you have spontaneously helped somebody who needed it. Sincerity is always in. My dictionary defines a nerd as a gauche, unsophisticated or uncool person. Hug your inner nerd today.

CHAPTER FIVE

CONNECT AND SHARE

"Humankind has not woven the web of life. We are but one thread within it. Whatever we do to the web, we do to ourselves. All things are bound together. All things connect."

Chief Seattle

1. Remember That It's All One Thing

Removing obstacles and giving ourselves the time and space to process our lives opens us to greater unity with life as a whole and with its countless forms. Each of us is soaked in this higher consciousness. We are sponges in an infinite ocean beyond imagining, most completely ourselves when we are soaked in the water. We function best when we operate according to this greater intelligence located inside and outside of us. Whether we feel it or not, whether we accept it or not, we're always in it and it's always in us. We are it. It is us.

The world's spiritual traditions recognize that our individual differences do not mean separation from each other. Acknowledging our unity, they teach openness and inclusion rather than division and exclusion. Jesus announced this unity of spirit that embraces all of us, teaching and demonstrating how to live it in daily life. He scandalized society by breaking down barriers between Jew and gentile, by welcoming women as equals and disciples, by focusing on children as worthy of God's concern and by welcoming the mentally and physically ill into the community as equals. He lived the spirit through applied love, which includes everybody.

Likewise, Buddha and other great spiritual teachers realized that understanding and serving the interdependence of all living things could change the character of our lives and transform the world. Accepting our basic equality and the necessity for compassion among all living things, their basic message is the same.

Christ tells us to do to others as we would have them do to us. Sikhs recognize no strangers, only friends. Taoism views our neighbour's gain and loss as our own gain and loss. Unitarianism respects the interdependent web of life. Jainism tells us we should treat all creatures as we would like to be treated. Islam teaches us to wish for others what we would wish for ourselves.

The traditions also tell us what not to do. Judaism teaches us not to do to our neighbour what is hateful for us. Hinduism, Buddhism, Confucianism and Zoroastrianism, in their own ways, see our duty as avoiding doing to others that which would bring pain if done to us. And Native spirituality says our completeness grows according to our relationship to the earth and other life forms, all manifestations of the Creator.

So there's a two-pronged reality involved. On the one hand, each of us is a unique person, with our own characteristics and gifts to share. On the other hand, we are all full and equal members of universal intelligence. Call it whatever you want – God, Tao, Creator or Brahman. We did not have to earn it. It just is.

I find this both liberating and appalling. It means we are not separated from anything. What do we do now?

We can start by being conscious of our membership in the big water and recognizing that, although we may often feel isolated, our borders do not end at our minds and bodies. We can step back from our fears, opinions and anxieties, pausing inwardly to catch everything in the act of being connected.

Relax and watch people being themselves without judging them or comparing yourself to them. Notice the ways that people try to do the right thing. Notice the pain they show behind their social masks. What are their best qualities? What are yours?

Observe the similarities and differences in the all-encompassing curiosity of a cat and the single-minded obsessions of a toddler. Stare at the blue sky, a raging fire, a long line of distant headlights at night. Get up early and watch the sun come up. Get off the couch and watch the sun go down. What are the differences in how these experiences make you feel? Notice when you feel lonely, when you feel connected and how easily you move from feeling to feeling.

Stand on a shore, listen to the water and look at the universe that exists below its surface. Stare until you begin to see the incredible diversity of life forms that interacts there. Crawlers, swimmers, floaters, green stuff waving like flags. Notice how orderly and serene it seems from up top. Imagine how it feels when that universe is disrupted by human feet or an all-terrain vehicle. Think about how various forms of life rely on each other for sustenance.

Reflect on your interdependence - how easily the order of your life could be changed by a belly laugh, an accident, a storm or a lottery win; a death, a birth, a chance meeting or the ending of a relationship. Remember times when you felt peaceful. Notice how a prayer shifts your mood. Do you feel most peaceful when you feel connected to something greater than you?

We consist of material matter and spiritual energy, two aspects of the same conscious process that is always happening everywhere. None of us owns it but it belongs to all of us. Giving ourselves the time and space to be still allows us to be more fully ourselves within this world of living intelligence. We are animated by the same intelligence that animates everything. In its midst, we are most ourselves when we are becoming ourselves.

2. Walk Your Path

Until a few centuries ago, a harmonious relationship with universal intelligence was considered essential to the well being of individuals and societies. Shamans, medicine men and other healers had the responsibility of restoring this harmony to the troubled and physically ill. People were well when they were whole. Being whole meant knowing your place in the universe and living in daily harmony with all of life.

Today we have countless material advantages but thirst for this connection. The time and energy we spend in meeting our obligations to consume and produce can leave us with little sense of the ultimate reality of our lives. We know *what* we are doing but its connection to the big picture can seem remote.

There is an old story with many versions [1] that speaks to the sense of isolation and uncertainty. It begins in a great desert through which people for centuries travelled, many dying, the lucky ones merely burdened with fear, fatigue and thirst. One day, about halfway across the desert, water came bubbling out of the ground and a clean, cold spring was born.

Beginning that day, the spring became a destination for travellers seeking to quench their thirst and bathe in the water. They found serenity and healing there, resuming their journeys with new strength and clearer purpose. Some left boulders of many colours and shapes as symbols of gratitude.

As the centuries passed, the boulders became larger, fancier and more numerous, piling so high that they covered the spring and left only one small entrance. Eventually, a special group of men and women appeared, wearing distinctive robes and speaking a strange language. They devised a set of rules for protecting the spring. They determined that, at certain times of the year, only those people who could afford to pay would be admitted.

Many wars were fought over who could and could not use the spring. In gratitude, the victors erected even more stones, finally making the spring unreachable. Travellers collapsed and died as the special guardians conducted their rituals in tribute to the monument of stones and the legend of the healing waters.

Over time, strange people arrived at the hidden spring, insisting that the barriers and its custodians be pulled away so that all people could drink from the water and purify themselves. These fanatics were honoured by some as prophets and persecuted by others as rebels. As time passed, so did they. But the legend lives on.

Stories of the spring have passed down to younger generations. Some have believed and some have not. But even today, in the dark of night, there are those who hide among the rocks and claim that, when their fear of the guards has subsided and the stillness in the air is just right, they hear echoes of the running water and smell the freshness of its healing spray.

Connecting to the life-giving spring of deeper consciousness means clearing boulders and rocks having many different shapes, sizes, colours and textures. It requires conscious living while we work, play, maintain relationships, worship, experience joy and endure suffering. Mediators can't do it for us but they can support our voyage of discovery by helping us to integrate the human and divine aspects of our personal experience.

Sometimes we find guides who help bring our life's journey closer to the water. Sometimes we find custodians who show us how to worship the rocks that cover the spring. We need to know the difference, so that we can distance ourselves from:

Any religious system which insists that the Creator loves every living thing while being bent on vengeance, punishment and destruction,

Any preachers who insist that only their spiritual beliefs and rules are correct and can never be questioned,

Any religious organization that insists on an elite class of people that is more worthy than others of God's love,

Any organization that justifies discrimination, hatred, violence and persecution against individuals, groups or other religions,

Any religious leaders who never acknowledge error or weakness and justify all their words and actions as God's will.

We can't complete our spiritual journey by remote control. We bear the responsibility for conducting it. Being fully human means accepting and recognizing our common humanity with others, including the people we dislike. Authentic guides can help us to see that finding our path is directly connected to helping others find their paths, through compassion, justice and kindness. And they can help us to learn that our existence has meaning, even when it seems unclear and remote. Becoming more conscious of a greater reality has less to do with obeying rules than with freeing ourselves to experience in our daily lives the mystery that wants to be discovered.

3. Recognize Your Teachers When You Meet Them

We learn from everywhere all the time - challenges, failures, successes, humorous situations, accidents, coincidences, people, other living things and sheer trickery. If we relax and see them as opportunities, our experiences can help us maintain a fresh view of the world and ourselves. If we load ourselves down with beliefs and attitudes intended to insulate us against change, we are more likely to learn the hard way - sometimes described as the one where what's right turns out to be what's left after we've done everything else wrong. Whether the lessons are harsh or pleasant, we learn best when we recognize our teachers and allow ourselves to be taught.

1. Significant people. Parents and grandparents teach us about the world and provide our first lessons in how to conduct ourselves in it. Key school teachers can help motivate us to pursue our dreams. Mr. Ted Jewell was my homeroom teacher in grade eight. He also taught music using a phonograph named Albert. Mr. Jewell had high standards but recognized each student as unique, with special gifts, and framed his expectations accordingly. To this day, many of us carry his influence as both an affirmation and a spur.

The occasional walk on the wild side can also make a difference in our lives. People who antagonize us and seem to get in our way can hold up a mirror, showing us places in ourselves that need attention. Unconventional people who seem eccentric at first glance may give us imaginative solutions and ideas.

2. Our failures. As long as we avoid taking ourselves too seriously, we can learn important lessons when we trip over ourselves. Even a reputation for wisdom can seduce us into self-importance that causes us to overlook the banana peel that life puts in our way to remind us that if wisdom isn't humble it isn't wisdom. When we accept without self-judgement the lessons that grow out of incorrect assumptions, impulsive acts and wrong choices, we make it easier to take responsibility and absorb the teaching. We reduce the chances of repeating the mistakes and put ourselves in better position to make creative choices stemming from the experience.

3. Meaningful coincidence. Synchronicities are seemingly accidental events that take place at just the right time. They spring from the unified energy field to which everything, including us, belongs. The chance meeting with someone you haven't seen in a long time, who happens to know someone who is looking to hire someone with your skills. The spur-of-the-moment decision to drive more slowly and turn right just before the washed-out highway that you could not see in the fog. The casual comment and shot of energy at the end of a conversation that prompts you to spend more time talking to someone who changes the perspective and direction of your life. The windfall that enables you to relieve a financial crisis. The book on the shelf that dominates your attention, demands that you take it home, then proceeds to alter your viewpoint. The animals whose characteristics most touch your emotions.

Each of us is exposed to these potentially life-changing developments and symbols, delivered to head, heart and body at the right time and in the strangest of places. We are more likely to learn from them if we pause long enough to absorb their messages and reflect on their meaning in our lives.

5. Spiritual teachers. Students bestow authority on teachers, living or deceased, by choosing them and accepting their teachings. We need to be careful in making these choices, especially if we are vulnerable to interpreting our compulsive wishes as inner voices. Our journeys require that we bestow authority only on teachers who have gained mastery and wisdom from their own experience and who are willing to open and inspire rather than control us. Authentic teachers:

Help us move away from the idea that we are sinful, unworthy children toward the realization that we are spiritual beings capable of transforming our lives,

Accept students with imperfections, recognizing that the capacity for good and evil, compassion and greed, wisdom and foolishness are always in us. They do not offer formulas to escape suffering. They help us incorporate pain's lessons into our life experience,

Recognize students' authority and do not require our unquestioning obedience. They happily provide tools that help us find our own paths,

Avoid pre-cooked formulas, methods and systems that promote imitation and lose their impact in real life,

Live the integrity of their teachings. But, imperfect like the rest of us, they can also be impatient pains in the butt and demonstrate a range of flaws. They may not be great communicators and their teachings may be incomplete. But if they help us move to more authentic living, they earn the respect and love that we give them.

Take a few minutes to reflect on teachers in your life. Write a few notes, capturing your first thoughts. Avoid over-analyzing them:

1. Make a list of five significant people in your life, past or present. What lessons have you learned from them? How have these lessons affected your life?

2. Which water, land or air animals most attract your attention? What do you like most about them? Which of their attributes or behaviours would you like to absorb?

3. Make a short list of coincidences that have come into your life over the last two months. How did they affect you? What messages did you receive? Notice coincidences in your life and think about what they mean to you.

4. List three people who have made you uncomfortable. What don't you like about them? Which of these characteristics do you possess or desire?

5. Who have been the spiritual teachers, alive or deceased, who have had the greatest impact on you? What have you learned from them that has influenced your life?

4. Dance With Fear

When we see ourselves as lucky, we see a connection between what we do and what happens to us. We use the tools at hand and move toward that which we were born to do - our destiny. Someone once commented to the great golfer Gary Player that he was lucky to be so successful at hitting golf balls out of sand traps. "Yeah.", Player responded, "And the more I practice, the luckier I get."

When we see ourselves as unlucky, we believe we have no control over what happens to us and are more likely to accept what we see as our unchangeable fate. Some people grow stronger from adversity, like those children who overcome abuse and poverty to succeed. Others bow to fear and frustration despite loving and privileged upbringings.

Carrying out the work necessary to fulfill our destiny involves confronting the conflict between the way things are and the way we want them to be. We need to be willing to leave our comfort zones for a while, trusting that our anxiety is temporary and that something new and better will be born out of our efforts. This is difficult to achieve when our energy is contaminated by a struggle with self-doubt and fear. Change works best on clean-burning fuel.

Healthy fear triggers a response that helps us defend ourselves against attack, flee a snarling dog or rescue someone from a burning house. Feeling vulnerable is a natural reaction when our job is threatened or when we adopt new ways of thinking in order to deal with unpredictable situations. But a lot of our fear is a trick that we play on ourselves.

We invent fear when we imagine, without any solid evidence, painful things that could happen in the future. Sometimes, instead of visualizing a particular disaster, we just carry a sick feeling around with us. Fear based on illusion multiplies itself into a kind of double whammy - fear that feeds on the fact that we are afraid. This is a long walk in a cold rain.

The power of the double whammy multiplies again if we buy the illusion that says we are supposed to be happy all the time. Feelings of happiness and tranquility are states through which we occasionally pass on our way to somewhere else. We cannot be dynamic individuals if we are always in a googly state of tranquility. We cannot adapt to life in the world unless we take action that is often clumsy and painful. Our lives consist of temporary states, both pleasant and unpleasant.

Much of the pain of fear comes from struggling against it. When we fight or hide from fear we set up an artificial self that is never supposed to be afraid - we cut ourselves off from who we really are. We end up fighting with ourselves. When we stop wrestling and accept the reality of fear, we can reduce our energy burden and put ourselves in better position to overcome its negative effects by relaxing into it more. Here are four ideas for dancing with fear:

1. Take it easy on yourself. Instead of fighting it, let fear co-exist with other emotions. Be aware of them all without judging yourself – they are your children and your guides. Out of the mouths of babes, you know? Fear, self-doubt and anger affect all of us and live alongside caring, courage and generosity. Accepting this reality can help us to understand who we really are. Practice staying in the present without imagining what could go wrong in the future.

2. Don't project fears onto others. One of the ways we re-direct the pain that comes from fear, self-doubt and anger is to project it onto other people. The resulting suspicions and misinterpretations keep the cycle going. By reducing our negative assumptions about others we can interrupt the cycle. Reflect on how suspicion or anxiety may influence you to take others' angry statements personally when they may simply reflect their own fears. A reduced sense of being under attack allows us to bring more positive energy to communicating with others.

3. Let go of obsolete fears. Let's face it, there are times when we must recognize personal weaknesses, difficult people and painful challenges that we've avoided. By working on these issues we can reclaim the creative energy and confidence that they have siphoned from us. As you commit yourself to confronting personal weaknesses, completing unpleasant tasks and communicating with difficult people, you can release your fears by expressing them to yourself, writing them out, sharing them with someone you trust or surrendering them to any universal power in which you believe. Although progress may seem slow and inconsistent, working on fears and releasing them from time to time helps to reduce their power in our lives, to increase belief in ourselves and to elicit support from universal intelligence based on the sincerity of our commitment.

4. Reflect on the origins of your fears. Recognizing fears and making a commitment to reducing their negative impact opens the door to discovering where they come from. You can do this alone, with a friend or with a qualified professional. Distinguish feelings based on actual threats from those that have arisen from your attitudes and beliefs about yourself and others. Thinking about times when self-doubts and fears were first planted in our lives can uncover hidden and valuable aspects of ourselves that, at some point, may have gone missing.

The direction of our lives is determined by the combination of where we choose to go and where life takes us. Our chances of being among those lucky people who move toward where they need to go increase when our bodies, minds and hearts commit themselves to the trip. This unity is strengthened when we trust and love ourselves enough to feel our fears as part of us and to let them go when their time has passed.

5. Make Your Goals Fit Your Purpose

Casey Stengel played major league baseball for many years and later managed the New York Yankees to repeated championships. This great teacher and leader said profound things in both simple and complicated ways. His teachings are not for framing on some wall of philosophy because reading them can give you brain cramps. Living them is the only way to understand them. Casey once said, " If you don't know where you're going, you might end up somewhere else. "

Goals identify what we want to achieve over a specific period of time. We can set them in any area of life: pass final exams, set aside enough time for the vacation, save five thousand dollars, learn how to turn on a computer, pay off the mortgage by 2007, write the book, run the mile in less than two hours, collect five boxes of canned goods for the food bank. We can set them for today, this week, this month, this season, this year and two, three or five years down the road.

Purpose is much bigger than goals. Purpose is a voyage of discovery. It incorporates all aspects of our lives into discovering who we really are as we make decisions about where we want to go and how we want to get there. We find clues to purpose in our greatest talents and personal challenges, those people and experiences that teach us most deeply, the causes that most elicit our compassion, coincidences and passionate involvement with things that we love so much that we lose track of time.

Sometimes our purpose seems clear to us and we can choose goals that best serve it. Assembling a volunteer team, collecting a truckload of clothing and depositing the clothes at the distribution depot are three goals that may fit the purpose of clothing the disadvantaged. Learning software programs a, b and c, putting together a good resume and winning over a key person are goals that can bring us closer to being paid for work that we love.

At other times our direction is less clear. We may feel confusion or a vague sense of being pulled to something that we can't quite make out. At these times, goals and favourite activities can act as vehicles that give us forward movement by introducing us to experiences that clarify our purpose down the road. Providing a sympathetic ear for people in crisis or cheering up the lonely may reflect a special ability and desire to elevate people's emotions. Simplifying computer instructions or complicated ideas may indicate a special gift for making information understandable so that more people can participate.

When goals and purpose fail to flow together in some way, an almost magical deception can undermine our sense of direction. If we concentrate on the goals outside of the gravitational pull of purpose, they may not take us where we intend or need to go. Obeying the dictates of goals for their own sake may keep us busy but it can also cut us off from the *why* that gives our efforts meaning. As Casey says, we might end up somewhere else.

Seeing our goals in relation to our sense of purpose enables us to more easily determine if we are on the right track and if our goals need adjusting. Goals are like the instruments on an airplane. If the purpose involves arriving at point a, the pilots must fly higher and lower, often shifting direction. They will move faster or slower depending on the wind and fuel supply. They will adapt to the nose and tail dancing in different directions. And sometimes they will be forced to land the aircraft at an unplanned destination, leaving passengers to finish the trip by bus.

The overriding intention stays the same but the steps must remain flexible. If the pilots focus on keeping all the instruments in the same position for the whole trip, they will not only miss their destination, they may well end up running out of fuel in the air or sinking into a river. The purpose of the voyage, rather than its instruments, defines its meaning and determines its process.

As your own pilot, you can move in directions that are most important for you by believing in yourself, trusting the process of your life and allowing yourself to move toward what pulls and energizes you. Here are four ideas for tapping into your sense of purpose.

1. Do not kill time. Know the difference between the instant gratification of cheap thrills and the fullness produced by experiences that support your passion and your need for energizing fun.

2. Review what you pay the most attention to. Chances are you dedicate most of your energies to these things. Which of them engage your passionate interests? Which of them drain you? Follow your passions away from the drainers.

3. Take a leap of faith. Identify a vision, an idea or a desire that attracts you and would improve your life or the lives of others. It can be big or small and apply to any area – relationships, social activities, self-care, work, fun, surroundings or making a difference in the world. State your commitment to moving toward it and release it to universal intelligence, asking for help. Start doing the work by making something happen. Let your goals and methods evolve from your vision and actions. Trust yourself and the process even if your goals are initially unclear.

4. Compare your purpose and most valued goals with those of your employer. Where do they complement each other? Where do they contradict each other? What can you do to maintain a pay cheque while fitting your work situation to your passions, best talents and sense of purpose?

When we commit ourselves to goals that carry out our purpose or move us toward it, our talents become unified and enriched - and so do we. This requires that we know our tolerance for goals and the difference between those that move us forward and those that kill time.

6. Give It Away

Now, I'm all in favour of good works. But concentrating too much on being virtuous worries me. I guess it's a matter of emphasis. *Virtue* is defined as general moral excellence, right action and thinking, and goodness of character. Strive to be virtuous, we are told, and we will develop character through good works. This is where it can get complicated.

When our main goal is virtue, we can become self-centred. The people we help can become stepping stones who enable us to climb onto self-made pedestals where we can display our virtue-osity to ourselves and to others. We can end up pursuing virtue as an impersonal end in itself. A short text from the Chinese sage Chuang Tzu captures the distinction between giving unconditionally and giving to pursue virtue. *In When Life Was Full There Was No History*, he says:

> *"In the age when life on earth was full, no one paid any special attention to worthy men, nor did they single out the man of ability... They were honest and righteous without realizing that they were ' doing their duty.' They loved each other and did not know that this was ' love of neighbour.' They deceived no one yet they did not know that they were ' men to be trusted.' They were reliable and did not know that this was ' good faith.' They lived freely together giving and taking, and did not know that they were generous."* [2]

In other words, they did the right thing because it needed doing. Chuang Tzu is telling us that the most important giving is unconditional and comes from the heart. Empathy is not the same as compassion. Empathy is a deeply sympathetic feeling for others. Compassion is the action we take when we feel empathy for them. Growing out of our own painful experiences (which shorten the distance between our pain and the pain of others), compassion can embody small acts of kindness or bold acts of determination. Either way, it moves us away from self-absorption and gives us a sense of working for the good of all.

The Grapes of Wrath is one of my favourite movies. Released in 1940, it depicts the Joad family's struggle to re-establish roots in California following the Dust Bowl's desolation of their lives in Oklahoma. There's a scene of loving kindness in an eatery where grandpa walks in with two grandchildren, a pre-teen girl and her younger brother. Grandma has gone to the toilet and the abused and overloaded truck that carries all of the family's belongings is loading up on gas and radiator water. Grandpa wants to buy a loaf of bread for a dime so that grandma, who has no teeth, can soften it in water and eat.

The hard-bitten waitress tells him the bread is for the eatery's sandwiches only and, besides, a loaf costs fifteen cents. Grandpa keeps trying and the waitress keeps brushing him off. Finally, the crusty owner says give him the bread. The waitress protests but brings out a loaf. Grandpa says would she mind splitting off a dime's worth, they have a thousand miles to go, they don't know if they'll make it but their money's organized tight to try. The waitress starts to protest but the owner says give him the whole loaf.

After paying his dime grandpa pauses on his way out as the children stare longingly at some candy bars in the display window of the counter. Grandpa has a penny left in his hand and asks the waitress how much for the candy. She hesitates, looks at the children and says two for a penny. He pays the penny, the children each get a big piece of candy and they all leave contented.

Two tough-looking truckers are eating at the counter. One says them ain't two-for-a-cent candies, them's nickel-apiece candies. The waitress says what's it to you and cleans the counter near the cash register. The other trucker says we're losing time and they get up to pay their bill. They leave big coins on the counter and walk to the door. As they open the door, the waitress says hey, wait, you got change coming! One of the truckers turns around and says, what's it to ya? The waitress looks at the coins, then at the departing men and says with a smile: truck drivers! The scene is unbearable in its pain and beauty.

Each of us participates in a constant process of giving and receiving that has an impact on our immediate surroundings and the flow of energy everywhere. Everything we think and do makes a difference. Compassionate and unconditional works best in lubricating the loop. And we get back more than we give. Here are four ideas for giving it away:

1. Commit random acts of ordinary kindness. It's like spreading peach pits wherever we go. We may never see any of the peaches and people on the receiving end may never know. We can be with people in their darkest hours, listening to their dreams and expressing faith in them with one sentence rather than a speech. We can plant ideas, visit an elder, bake extra and share. We can be peacemakers in an argument, buy from local merchants, go outside and get to know the neighbours.

We can put an arm around somebody who looks like they need it. Pick up litter, fix something even if we didn't break it, talk with the mail carrier. Feed a cat, plant a tree, take children to the park, teach somebody how to read, ride a bike or shoot a basketball. Collect cans to raise money so kids can swim in a safe place. Change the toilet paper for everybody, not just ourselves.

2. Share gifts and abundance. There's more than enough for all of us in the universal soup and we all deserve some. Economic systems steer more material goods to some people than to others. We can influence the flow according to how we share our gifts and abundance.

We all have passionate interests, special talents and creative abilities. Sharing them freely rather than begrudgingly gives others what they need on their paths, helps each of us to carry out our unique purpose in life and stimulates the circulation of giving and receiving by providing inspiration for others to do the same. Whether they involve people, information or things, our gifts and abundance attain their full meaning when we put them out there.

3. Be available to others. Giving other people our full attention is both an obvious thing to write and more difficult than it reads. It boils down to showing conscious interest in others' concerns without distraction, rather than waiting impatiently for our turn to speak or being compulsively clever when we do speak. It begins with listening and radiates out to minimizing conversational self-references, avoiding self-importance and paying attention to unspoken cries for help. It means having confidence in what we are saying, sharing positive attitudes, getting to the point and telling the truth kindly. If we do it right we feel lighter at the end and our preoccupations and pretensions get a little weaker.

4. Say thanks. Saying thanks completes the cycle and stimulates its continuation in new directions. We express gratitude for what we receive in many ways. We say grace over a meal. We look up thankfully when a family member avoids injury or worse. We express appreciation for the kindness of others. Every day we breathe, eat, laugh, enjoy the warmth of sunshine and are blessed by family and friends.

Expressing sincere gratitude for what we are able to give away can change our lives. According to Meister Eckhart, thank you is the only prayer we need to know. Saying thanks for something different every day can alter our consciousness by making us more sensitive to the immeasurable blessings that we encounter in every moment.

The opportunity to participate in the cycles of giving and receiving is a gift that allows us to discover our place in the small and big picture, and to help others do the same. Our job involves doing the right thing because it needs doing. Virtue can take care of itself.

7. Nobody Owns the Future: Make a Difference.

The richest five hundred people on the planet now control more wealth than the poorest three billion. Not all of our problems stem from greed, of course. But the high visibility of poverty, war, environmental degradation and human persecution stemming from this imbalance can overwhelm us. George Carlin once observed that nature is working on flushing us out like a bad fungus so that the planet can function the way it was meant to. Were we to stay on this path, there would eventually be only one pot-bellied mogul left, sipping the last of his champagne on a terrace overlooking the burned-out ruins of Desolation Boulevard.

We can doubt our ability to make a difference. We may feel numbed by our own anger, sorrow, fear and the sheer scope of the problems. The danger of getting used to this state lies in the possibility that it will evolve into learned helplessness - wishing that something could be done about something and not doing something about it. We can get trapped in a circle where we accept the degradation of living things as inevitable and spend too much of our energies fearing what we feel we cannot change.

We can avoid this trap by trusting the process of our lives to lead us toward opportunities for addressing problems and expressing our truth in the world. As individuals, groups and communities, we can help enrich life and alleviate pain starting now. We can protect life, support social justice, oppose injustice, build community harmony and the inner life of individuals, give the disadvantaged a fair chance and protect society's social support systems. Our choices and actions count immediately and into the future.

My friend John Butler says that many of the forces that we fear are born in a hollow and forbidding place he calls The Hole In The Middle Of Everything (THITMOE). [3] He says that, as individuals and as societies, we always have the choice to deal with the Hole in one or more ways according to our individual nature, whether that means fighting it, understanding it, filling it with love or exposing it.

Regardless of which roles are most natural for us in addressing the Hole, we can start by finding something that we want to do something about and doing something about it. If we take a look around we can discover causes that fit our sense of compassion or anger, and that can benefit from the talents we enjoy using, whether we use them up front or behind the scenes and whether they relate to people, information or things

The full impact of pursuing the goals of a cause can't be predicted. We will learn many lessons, some the hard way. But we will also experience much success by happy accident. Rippling into the big water, our efforts will affect life in unknown ways. This applies to the work of mass movements, marginal groups and individuals alike. Who would have predicted in 1935, when a newly-sober Bill Wilson helped a supposedly hopeless alcoholic named Bill Smith, that Alcoholics Anonymous and a new approach to personal change would be born? And how do we measure the effects of the other ripples it continues to send into the big water?

While social, environmental and political degradation of the earth seem to worsen daily, support for organizations devoted to sustaining life also grows daily. This may be easy to overlook because there are thousands of such organizations and they do not fly under one banner. One day these organizations, as well as caring individuals working on their own, will create a world where, in order to survive and flourish, economics and technology will have to create conditions that nurture life in all its forms, including the civil societies that support them.

The efforts that make the difference will come from our individual decisions to stand for something and from the awareness that working for the well-being of others provides us with the opportunity to clarify our beliefs, gain knowledge and discover strengths that we may not have known we possessed. Life will be preserved and enhanced when we accept that there is no separation between helping others and finding our own voices. A kind word, a helping hand and a refusal to ignore injustice go a long way in the universal soup.

AFTERWORD

"You're never as good as you look when you're winning, and you're never as bad as you look when you're losing."

Earl Weaver

I once heard a friend say, "I only worry when it's time to worry." I was struck by the healthy irreverence and courage reflected in the statement. Whether we like it or not and regardless of our degree of enlightenment, it's in the nature of our journey to move between order and chaos, somberness and laughter, wisdom and foolishness. A healthy dose of irreverence – toward ourselves and toward the world – can keep us from tripping over excess seriousness and enable us to learn our lessons with more lightness.

The book has looked at the importance of pausing once in a while to update ourselves on what we want from life and on what life wants from us. I mentioned in the introduction that it is intended as a kind of companion, a resource to serve the reader's experience. It will probably work best if you include some chuckles and belly laughs along the way. I hope that you find the book useful in helping you align your outer activities with your inner voice.

NOTES

Chapter One

1. Neil Postman, *Amusing Ourselves to Death: Public Discourse in the Age of Show Business* (New York: Penquin Books U.S.A., Inc., 1992), pp. vii-viii.

2. Kalle Lasn and Bruce Grierson, "Malignant Sadness" , *Adbusters*, June-July, 2000, p.35.

3. Fritjof Capra, *The Turning Point: Science, Society and the Rising Culture* (New York: Simon and Schuster, 1992), p.188.

Chapter Two

1. Shunryu Suzuki, *Zen Mind, Beginner's Mind: Informal Talks on Zen Meditation and Practice* (New York: Weatherhill, Inc., 1970), p.54.

Chapter Three

1. J. Krishnamurti, *The Awakening of Intelligence* (New York: Avon Books, 1973), pp. 63-66.

Chapter Four

1. John Butler, *Office Décor* (Personal correspondence).

2. Viktor Frankl, *Man's Search For Meaning* (New York: Simon and Schuster, 1959).

3. Frederick Lenz, *Surfing the Himalayas: A Spiritual Adventure* (New York: St. Martin's Press, 1995), pp.176-207.

4. John G. Neihardt, *Black Elk Speaks: Being the Life Story of a Holy Man of the Oglala Sioux* (New York: William Morrow and Co., 1932), p.195.

Chapter Five

1. Tom Harpur, *For Christ's Sake* (Toronto: Oxford University Press, 1986), pp. 1-3.

2. Thomas Merton, *The Way of Chuang Tzu* (Boston: Shambhala Publications, Inc., 1965), pp. 114-115.

3. John Butler, *The Hole In The Middle Of Everything* (Personal correspondence).

SOURCES & SELECTED BIBLIOGRAPHY

The following list includes this book's sources as well as selected books and articles by exemplars, guides and teachers. They are provided for readers who may wish to explore the themes more deeply.

BOOKS

A Course in Miracles. Second Edition. Combined volumes, including text, teachers' manual and workbook. Foundation for Inner Peace. New York: Penguin Books U.S.A., Inc., 1996.

Adrienne, Carol. *The Purpose of Your Life.* New York: William Morrow and Company, Inc., 1998.

Aslett, Don. *Clutter's Last Stand.* Cincinnati: Writer's Digest Books, 1984.

Cahill, Thomas. *Desire of the Everlasting Hills.* New York: Anchor Books, 1999.

Campbell, Joseph. *The Hero With a Thousand Faces.* Princeton, New Jersey: Princeton University Press, 1949.

Capra, Fritjof. *The Turning Point.* New York: Simon and Schuster, 1982.

Chopra, Deepak. *The Seven Spiritual Laws of Success.* San Rafael, California: Amber-Allen Publishing and New World Library, 1993.

Covey, Stephen R., A. Roger Merrill and Rebecca R. Merrill. *First Things First.* New York: Simon and Schuster, 1994.

Fawcett, Brian. *Cambodia: A Book For People Who Find Television Too Slow.* Vancouver: Talonbooks, 1986.

Frankl, Viktor. *Man's Search For Meaning.* New York: Simon and Schuster, 1959.

Gleick, Jim. *Faster: The Acceleration of Just About Everything*. New York: Viking Books, 1999.

Goldberg, Natalie. *Long Quiet Highway: Waking Up in America*. New York: Bantam Books, 1993.

Hunt, Diane, and Pam Hiatt. *The Tao of Time*. New York: Simon and Schuster, 1991.

Krishnamurti, J. *The Awakening of Intelligence*. New York: Avon Books, 1973.

Le Guin, Ursula K. *Tao Te Ching*. Boston: Shambhala Publications, Inc., 1998.

Lenz, Frederick. *Surfing the Himalayas: A Spiritual Adventure*. New York: St. Martin's Press, 1995.

Merton, Thomas. *The Way of Chuang Tzu*. Boston: Shambhala Publications, Inc., 1965.

Myss, Carolyn. *Anatomy of the Spirit*. New York: Random House, Inc., 1996.

Neihardt, John G. *Black Elk Speaks*. New York: William Morrow and Co., 1932.

Nhat Hahn, Thich. *The Miracle of Mindfulness*. Boston: Beacon Press, 1975.

Postman, Neil. *Amusing Ourselves to Death*. New York: Viking Penguin, Inc., 1985.

Postman, Neil and Steve Powers. *How To Watch TV News*. New York: Penquin Books, U.S.A. Inc.,1992.

Rybczynski, Witold. *Waiting For the Weekend*. New York: Viking Penguin, Inc., 1991.

Sams, Jamie. *Dancing the Dream*. San Francisco: Harper Collins Books, 1999.

Servan-Shrieber, Jean-Louis. *The Art of Time*. Reading, Massachusetts: Addison-Wesley Publishing Company, Inc., 1988.

Steinbeck, John. *The Grapes of Wrath*. New York: Bantam Books, 1939. Also a movie, directed by John Ford (1940).

St. James, Elaine. *Living the Simple Life*. New York: Hyperion, 1996.

Storr, Anthony. *Solitude*. London: Fontana Paperbacks, 1988.

Suzuki, Shunryu. *Zen Mind, Beginner's Mind*. New York: Weatherhill, Inc., 1970.

Watts, Alan. *The Wisdom of Insecurity*. New York: Pantheon Books, 1951.

ARTICLES

Csillag, Ron. The Reciprocity of Entreaty. *The Toronto Star* (September 29, 2001).

Grierson, Bruce. Headrush. *Adbusters*, No. 25 (Spring, 1999) .

Just Quit: The Fine Art of Breaking Free. *Utne Reader*, No. 77 (October, 1996). A section featuring several articles on how to disengage from the rat race and create a life that makes sense.

Lasn, Kalle and Bruce Grierson. Malignant Sadness. *Adbusters*, No. 30 (June/July, 2000) www.adbusters.org.

Moody, Ron. Too Cool For Cool. *Gentlemen's Quarterly* (June, 1999).

Slow Down. *Utne Reader*, No. 80 (March-April, 1997). A section featuring several articles on finding our natural rhythm in a speed-crazed world.

ISBN 1553958840-5

9 781553 958840